BIU JEE

Wing Chun Mastery

JASON KOROL

Martial Way Press

BIU JEE

Wing Chun Mastery

JASON KOROL

Martial Way Press

To Carmella Marie. You taught this fella to live with his whole heart, motivated by reverent awe of God and love, not envy or fear. All those lessons and all that love that you poured into me are what put me on this path. All who study with me will always get a piece of your heart and soul too.

"Biu Jee, or Thrusting Fingers, is the power of Wing Chun and is the final hand form learned...taking place in the advanced stage of training. After the student has learned to control the fighting environment in his prior training, Biu Jee teaches how to become a highly unorthodox fighter able to attack from any angle with devastating power, and able to operate in any situation. A competent Biu Jee practitioner can't be taken by surprise and is able to fight from any position."

Sifu Tony Massengill via Grand Master Ip Ching &
Master Edmond Fong

Introduction

Why forms? Because there's no way to know what changes await us in the future. No one should be more aware of the dangers of the normalcy bias than a martial artist. Circumstances can change in startling ways. The environmental and tactical variances of violence, if we're serious about our studies, must be given their due because history is full of dead and/or defeated people who thought, "that'll never happen." Oddly enough, to be prepared for an uncertain future we must revisit the past. And we must never be so vain and self-satisfied as to discard the timeless lessons passed down to us, for in them are keys to understanding and, indeed, performance.

In other words, to be prepared for an enemy and environment that can change rapidly, without warning, requires that we not trade simplicity for comprehensiveness. The realist and idealist are, in the martial arts, one and the same because though we must be prepared for brutal simplicity under pressure, we must be equally prepared for the unexpected. Thus it is with Wing Chun and its final form, Biu Jee. The simple fundamentals of the earlier forms work...but they're not *all* that work.

Many people today utterly misunderstand the Wing Chun forms for the same reason that they misapprehend the past. Wing Chun grew in the soil of a land vastly different than our own. It's difficult for us, with our air-conditioning and the ability to call 9-1-1, to truly comprehend the nature of a martial art in the mid-19th century in war-torn China (the Taiping Rebellion, incidentally, saw over 20 million deaths). The average American thinks "legalistically" rather than martially. That is to say, we consider the legal system and our lawyers when we think of combat. Close-range lethality and martial art training are, in most modern minds, separate issues. To paraphrase a great movie villain, Bane, "success has defeated us." Indeed, insofar as violence is concerned, civilization and technology are merely window dressing. Man, the sinner, is the cosmic rebel who insists on living by his own moral law rather than the transcendent one, and it's this that fine clothes and culture merely hides. History is, indeed, long in tales of shocking barbarity.

Thus, it's easy, and dangerous, to miss the larger point. *Are you a human weapon?* What good is it for 9-1-1 to exist if you've already been murdered? Does it matter to you - in your grave - that your murderer is convicted of the crime? The abstraction - *society* - certainly benefits from the functioning legal system; the dead fella… not so much.

If society starts to fall apart tomorrow, if there's some type of social collapse, what will we think of our martial arts then? And, truth be told, a man (or men) breaking into your house is a "private" social collapse, isn't it? That your neighbors are being attacked as well changes nothing about the reality of *your* assault. We ask the reader to respect this salient fact and keep it in mind. The masters of old who passed down a fighting system such as Wing Chun, and a form like Biu Jee, did it with the intent to live logically in a violent world. To study a form is to study a philosophy of violence; it's a degree in applied physics, combat theory, tactics, and self-defense ethics. To study it merely for the movements is to altogether miss the point and, we contend, dishonor the past.

Also, it's a colossal mistake to think that a form like Biu Jee, originating as it did over a century ago, isn't relevant to today's combat. Some people claim that this is the case and to justify the flawed logic they say something like, "imagine a soldier today going to war carrying a musket." The problem with this bit of baloney is that the human body we use to defend ourselves hasn't undergone any changes in that same time frame comparable to firearm technology. With the exception of many of us being, rather unfortunately, thicker around the midsection, of course. Like me and you, Leung Jan and Ip Man had two arms and two legs, so it's irrelevant - a categorical fallacy - to think that machine guns have altered this fact.

To that end, the true "traditionalist" isn't the one who ignorantly plays dress-up and regards any deviation of tactics or application as outright blasphemy, but the one who understands and respects the heart and soul of what their ancestors faced in a harsh world.

That said, in your hands is a book on Wing Chun's third and final empty hand form. Like the other forms, there are a million lessons to be learned and applied and no book can possibly capture all of them. We've sought to present to you, the reader and student, certain essentials that if absent will render the form useless. Or even worse than useless. The third form is third for a reason. It stands atop the foundation of the two previous forms, Siu Lim Tao and Chum Kiu, so we would be remiss to simply start here. It's an easy mistake to make in our day. But a mistake nevertheless. I should hope not to cost myself sales in the event that one is reading this as a sample, yet the truth of the matter is that this material is hardly helpful outside the rest of the context which the previous forms present. Starting with Biu Jee is like booking a honeymoon suite when you don't even have a girlfriend yet (although there's something to be said for that level of optimism). Wing Chun is an integrated package and to get from it what Biu Jee intends presupposes the entirety of the system.

We also note that the essentials of this form are just as important, if not absolutely critical, as those of the previous forms. Other lineages may or may not agree but we believe quite ardently that the absence of Biu Jee's heart and soul, much less the technical detail itself, is catastrophic for our comprehension and application of Wing Chun. It's for that reason that the author's main goal has been to present in this volume not only the technical details but also the *Sum Faat* - that is, the *heart-law* of the form. The proper mind of the thing is as important as the thing itself. We've said it in other writings but it bears repeating: we seek the logical integration of theory and practice. This is what it means to say "mind and body." The true martial artist is the man or woman of both - the integrated being, the fighter and the philosopher. To dispute this is to contradict oneself in a most awful way as it's to claim that one is either/or. It's to say that one is not a lover of wisdom but a de-facto brute and ignoramus. Or, on the other hand, that one is unwilling to defend life and rights. We assume that each martial artist sees the need and the beauty of being both, and it's exactly this which makes us martial artists in the first place.

Thus, it's to you that this is written: men and women of the mind and the fist; to those who love peace and hate war, but are prepared for it. Biu Jee provides the dedicated student both blazing firepower and tactical realism. Serious study of it yields the true fruit of excellence in the fighting method and the wisdom not to be bound by that method! It is literally what Bruce Lee had in mind when he encouraged his followers to have no way as way. He meant excellence and adaptability, not slavish adherence to the past, nor incompetence either.

With that said, we present to you the Biu Jee form of Wing Chun Kuen Sum Faat.

Biu Jee & Dr. Winchester

In the old sitcom, *M.A.S.H.*, there was a surgeon, Dr. Charles Emerson Winchester, who came to the show after the much-maligned Frank Burns character departed. Winchester, unlike the vain, vacuous and comically incompetent Burns, was a highly educated, cultured, and above all, gifted surgeon. Burns, you see, had been quite a hack. A pompous hack.

The thing is, though, Winchester, for all his superlative surgical skill, was no longer in a Boston hospital doing careful civilian surgery. No. He was in that awful war theatre of Korea during the early 1950's.

As it went, Winchester had an ego to match his impressive medical skills. He loved the fact that he was good at what he did. Up until that point in the show, Alan Alda's *Hawkeye Pierce*, the lady-loving, wise-cracking, Chief Surgeon of the *4077 Mobile Army Surgical Hospital* (M.A.S.H.) was the undisputed champion of doctors. Suddenly, Winchester appeared and his superior surgical skill was beyond doubt. A flustered Hawkeye asked, "what's so good about him?" Winchester replied,

"I do one thing at a time. I do it very well. Then I move on."

He was technically superior. He knew it. He loved it…that is, being better than everyone else.

Ah, but lest you begin to wonder what all this has to do with Wing Chun, it's exactly here that Winchester experiences his first true challenge of the war. When casualties rolled in to the M.A.S.H they came in a blood red tidal wave. Young boys all shot up, gored and mangled by bullets and artillery. On buses. On choppers. On the back of jeeps. They kept coming. And they all needed to be surgically repaired as quickly as possible so that other boys didn't die while waiting. (Despite being a goofball comedy in many ways, M.A.S.H nevertheless let it be known how terribly true it is that war is hell.)

They called it *"meatball surgery."* A great chef isn't needed in a fast-food chain, nor is a great surgeon's talent in a killing field.

Well, when Winchester experienced this for the first time, the "lesser" doctors, all of them used to the frantic pace of mass casualty surgery, worked with skillful haste. They patched them up and moved on. Winchester's mantra of doing one thing at a time very well, had this great weakness in a war-zone: it took too much time. Being too careful and too *skillful* with one boy might very well kill another two or three. That was/is the hard math of the war zone hospital and the battlefield. The other doctors warned him. They told him to hurry up. But the superior man's ego couldn't fathom that he was the problem. No. Winchester, used to accolades, awards, and awe, not rebuke, simply couldn't process how these inferior men could dare be critical of him!

At last, before someone died, an order had to be given that Hawkeye replace Winchester on a patient. It had to be done. Life was in the balance. The big goal - the preservation of life - trumped the niceties of convention.

The blow to Winchester's ego was enormous.

Gradually, of course, Winchester adapted to his new reality. He made adjustments despite how offensive the whole place was to his aristocratic sensitivities - in all its mud, grime, hurry and haste.

Biu Jee is the anti-Winchester form.

Biu Jee reminds technicians and professors that fighting is hell.

Biu Jee is Ulysses S. Grant in his muddy boots and hamper-ready uniform over against the perfectly put together, but battle-reticent, McClellan. McClellan, on paper, was said to be America's Napoleon. Lincoln replaced him with the "lesser man" who had none of the accolades. Why?

"This man fights," Lincoln said.

Biu Jee is the mud-splashed off-road vehicle compared to the perfectly kept sports car in the garage without a single crumb on the floor. A fight isn't about perfection; it's about skillful survival. Look good doing something else. Survive right now.

When someone is trying to kill you, when all that stands in the way of life or death, safety or serious injury, technical precision is not, repeat not, one's highest order. The law of the classroom gives way to the law of battle. Survive. Man is a curiously vain thing… supposedly the "animal of reason" but shot-through with contradiction and pride. He creates a fighting method designed to save his life but then turns the method itself into the thing to be saved and sacrifices his life unto it! Biu Jee, if we'll have the courage and intellectual consistency to see it, neither obliterates the core principles of Wing Chun *nor does it allow us to think that those principles are the point of the whole thing either.*

This amazing vehicle we have must be driven in the mud and the snow and the dust, over the hills, through the stream, across the rocks. Trying not to get our toys dirty means we don't have toys - they have us.

And that's exactly why many Wing Chun "purists" don't like it and/or don't understand it (Biu Jee, that is).

We can be like Winchester. We can obsess about our technical precision, sipping our metaphorical martial tea with our pinky in the air while our enemy beats the dickens out of us. Fighting is meatball surgery. It's a crisis unlike any other wherein brutal simplicity and adaptation are paramount. Biu Jee tells us that hard truth which is that we must get real or get gone. The system of Wing Chun is not more important than the reality that the system seeks to understand. The goal is not the system itself.

And that's the thing about systems altogether, incidentally. We need them in order to think rationally and truly about reality. But human pride is forever lurking. It's the primordial sin. And in our pride (as well as our deep-rooted desire for security) we make systems of truth the truth itself...at least we try to. But reality always gets the last laugh.

Okay, all that said, ready? Here we go...

Biu Jee Section 1: Blinding Them With Science

Biu Jee Section One looks deceptively easy. But far from just being a form where we're weirdly wiggling our fingers around, the main idea is to make sure that we study the craft of eye attacks from every conceivable angle and position. A blinded opponent is either finished entirely or greatly diminished. For this reason alone the smart self-defender makes eye-attacks - whether they be spears, gouges, rakes, or quick pokes - the primary thing. Also important to remember is that the early Wing Chun fighters, as well as all masters from that era in the past, whether Hakka or Cantonese in origin, were highly conditioned. Using eye attacks with an "unsharpened" tool, that is to say, a weak hand with brittle fingers, is foolish. The Biu Jee student, therefore, takes hand and finger conditioning seriously enough so as to sharpen their weapon and be capable of both severely injuring the targets (whether throat or eyes, incidentally) *and* withstanding accidental contact with harder objects should their attack be blocked and/or miss.

Starting position. Relax. Regulate your breathing and clear your mind. Normally at this point you'll draw a deep breath and release shoulder or other tensions as you exhale. Fighting (and life too) is stressful. Wing Chun training helps teach us how to deal with pressure and stress. It's easy to just zip past the form's opening in order to get on to the "important stuff." But failure to learn how to relax (and to breathe properly) under pressure and/or during conflict will assuredly cause us difficulties in life. Certainly, it's ruined many lives too. So, take a moment and take the deep breath. Take as many as you need. Slow down. Calm down. Take control. This is a critical lesson we all need to learn and practice. If we don't practice controlling our emotions they will control us. That's never a good thing. Ive never lost my temper and solved a problem and I'm sure you haven't either. Likewise, I've never hidden from an issue (due to fear or anxiety) and had it go away all by itself. Martial art training is always about conquering the first enemy: ourselves and our lack of discipline. Only then can we focus on the external enemy.

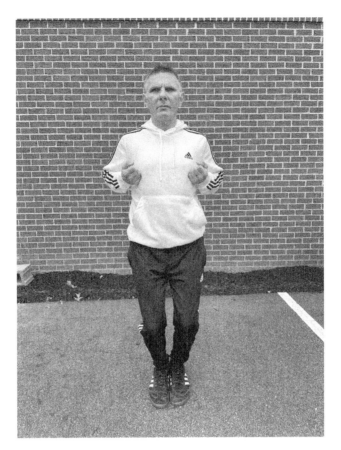

As with the other forms, drop your weight until your knees reach your toe-line. This forms the lower perimeter of your basic stance and teaches you how much your knees, as a general rule, should be bent while fighting. There are exceptions to this, yes, but this is the foundational rule. The Wing Chun forms are a master class of proper biomechanics, so don't skip this very important step. While sinking, be sure to keep your upper body in place, not slouching. Your trunk is like a camera on a tripod in the YJKYM.

With your weight in the front of your heels, turn your toes
outward.

Grip the ground with your toes and without disturbing
your upper body position, grip with your toes and push
your heels out. Your hips sink down and forward and
you're now in the Yi Ji Kim Yueng Ma (character two goat-
gripping stance).

. . .

With snappy smoothness, push your hands down via elbow power.

Lift your hands - they'll cross as they raise - via elbow power. Biu Jee, built upon the foundation of the previous forms, should be played with loose, snappy power in its actions.

Pull back swiftly and with power to the YJKYM training stance. At first, using powerful actions at high speed might cause you some balance problems but with practice it'll become second nature. Though Biu Jee looks just like Siu Lim Tao up until this point, you're doing these actions with explosive power, which wasn't the case as you first learned the material.

Use your elbow to drive your fist into the center-line launch position.

Execute the basic straight punch. We should never dismiss the efficacy of a good punch in the nose, nor get bored reviewing and practicing the essentials.

Thrust your fingers directly forward with short, snappy, shock power. The elbow should provide a little jolt to the action without fully extending the arm. A good Wing Chun fighter is developing "coiled spring" power…short burst power that's derived from good form (good structure) and relaxation. Though the eye is a primary target for this shocking weapon, the throat is also vulnerable.

Utilizing "long bridge" or extended power, snap your fingers quickly and powerfully downward. Practicing this action economically (with little arm movement, if any at all) prepares the Wing Chun fighter to attack the eyes or throat with sufficient power to assure injury to the foe.

Snap your fingers upward with economical and snappy power. This is a deceptively simple looking action but it takes years to master. Wing Chun forms, properly understood and practiced, are like an invaluable coach with years of experience. In this case we're being told by "the coach" not to forget the importance of attacking the eyes of the enemy - and to practice hitting them from a variety of clinch or bridge positions.

Repeat the action downward a second time. A good Wing Chun fighter prioritizes eye attacks. The Biu Jee form lets us practice snappy power from differing angles because during infighting it's quite likely that the opponent will move his head. Thus, it's highly important to develop this skill.

Biu Jee

As before, snap the fingers upward while keeping the arm
as still as possible.

For the third time, snap the fingers downward.

Complete the section by snapping the fingers upward for the third time.

After three up and down actions, turn you fingers inward from the upward position. There's no need to snap them into this position as it's the "launch" position for the ensuing "in/out" actions.

Snap your fingers outward and to the left. As with the up-down actions, focus the energy to the fingertips and keep the rest of the arm as still as possible.

Snap the fingers back to the inside position.

Repeat the action to the outside and left. We usually pause momentarily between the actions so as to make sure the energy is used properly. That said, it's perfectly okay to perform the action in quick succession too. The idea of forms is to produce mechanical proficiency and not to make you a slave to one particular way of doing them.

Snap your fingers back to the inside. We certainly aren't going to impress anyone when performing this section of Biu Jee and that's one of the beauties of Wing Chun. It's designed to keep us good looking after a fight rather than before it.

To the outside one last time. The fact that we do this three times shows its importance. Being able to attack the eyes from any position is a key survival component in all-out combat and not to be taken lightly.

Back to the inside for the last time. This completes the eye-rake section. Some families/lineages use this section as a defensive action rather than eye jabs/rakes. That's a valid interpretation and it's perfectly fine to train it that way. Our belief is that the defensive action of the extended arm is practiced in the Mook Jong form (section four). That being the case, we believe that it's best to practice the Biu Jee form in this manner or else there'd be no other practice of it in all the Wing Chun forms. As always, we're the most logical Wing Chun lineage but we don't like to brag. Just kidding. Consider all options and ideas and make the best decision you can. Wing Chun is for you and not the other way around. What good is a self-defense system in the hands of a man or woman who hasn't learned to think logically and for themselves? The worst blindness isn't due to eye jabs but to us if we're blinded by our own thoughtless allegiance.

Flip the hand over into the Taan-sao position with relaxed, snappy power.

Complete a Huen-sao (circling hand) by rotating your hand in a clockwise direction.

Complete the Huen-sao with a powerful grab, thereby
closing the fist. You've done this action countless
times throughout your training in the previous forms,
so it should be second nature by now and you can
add snap and power without compromising your form
or getting stiff. As always, we want snappy power.

Execute a Lop-sao with speed and power. At a high level - Biu Jee level - we should make no distinction between relaxation and power. Many people confuse "internal" and "external" power; they consider them as opposites. In fact, relaxation, clarity of mind (purpose), and good form yield the fruit of explosive energy.

REPEAT this sequence with the right side and then you're done with the opening section.

Side views for further clarification:

Notice the relaxed posture in the Sout Kune (chambered fist) position. Sifu Jason's elbows are naturally in line with his heels, giving him a triangular base. If the elbows are pulled back in a tight straight line it disconnects the elbow from the basic YJKYM structure. Also, it adds tension to the shoulder. Notice also that his hips are slightly forward and he's not slouching. During a fight, especially when infighting, a slight crouch is necessary in order to make one a smaller target. Nevertheless, the purpose of a form is to develop neuromuscular expertise (good mechanics). Be sure not to slouch when in the YJKYM.

With all this talk about attacking the eyes, let's not forget the importance and primacy of the backbone of Wing Chun, which is the trusted straight punch. The elbow drives the fist into the center, the fist is straight, knuckles facing the target and you're ready to fire the *jik kuen* right down the center.

There's a slight upward snap of the wrist at the end of the punch. This is "last second energy." Dempsey talked about this in his seminal boxing book, *Championship Fighting: the Art of Aggressive Defense*. The straight punch, like Dempsey's "left jolt" is the workhorse of a rational fighting science because it can be thrown with alarming power, swiftness, and accuracy. Learning to punch properly is becoming a lost art - if it hasn't already. Whereas the eyes are primary targets, so is the nose and face. The eyes are smaller targets than the rest of the face, and the fingers don't provide as large a weapon as the fist. Thus, in our advocacy for eye attacks, let's not forget that the straight punch should not be abandoned. Accuracy is always hard to come by in any fight, so don't rashly assume that eye jabs will solve all your problems. There are smart-cuts, but no short-cuts to success.

. . .

A side view of the downward finger rake. Notice that even at range, the arm is not fully locked out. It's almost fully extended but not totally. We also note, in light of what we just said about the straight punch, that much of Wing Chun's eye attack system is done from the clinch due to the issue of accuracy. This is a point that's often lost. Infighting in a life-or-death struggle is a vicious thing. Many Wing Chun students wrongly treat Chi-sao practice as a kind of hyper-technical game of "gotcha" when, in fact, it's all about learning scientific control of the bridge. In other words, control their balance while attacking and defending the weakest targets.

Sifu Jason plays the upward eye attack with his arm in a middle position. It's certainly acceptable to hold the arm higher when practicing this section if you prefer. At range (non-bridge contact distance) the eye jab, straight punch and kick are Wing Chun's primary tools. During infighting, however, we must develop a diversity of short range tools that can attack from any angle due to the variety of positions that present themselves. These attacks (eyes rakes, gouges, and jabs) must be practiced AND integrated into the rest of the Wing Chun systematic. Nothing is an end in and of itself.

3

Biu Jee Section Two - Kop Jarn

At close range there are a multitude of positions that present themselves. It's a critical error to think that infighting will be exactly like Chi-sao just as it's also a mistake to eschew Chi-sao for a strictly grappling system. Wing Chun is a striking system that grapples; a grappling system that strikes. In a real fight, *bridge contact* with the enemy is pushing, pulling, striking, kicking, breaking, locking, and throwing. It's all hands on deck. A great error is an over-reliance on the chain-punch due to the limited line-access it has, and the reality that the enemy will be moving. For this reason, not only do eye-rakes become necessary and formidable, but elbow strikes too.

Begin by lifting your hand near your ear. Watch your balance because you're going to go for a ride now. The "circle elbow" is going to go over the top as you turn completely to the right side.

Point the tip of the left elbow toward the right side as you turn quickly. An elbow strike is a fearsome tool. If you land it accurately it's a powerful weapon that has immense cutting capability.

At the completion of the turn, your right hand is in the chambered
position and your elbow has come all the way over the top. Be careful
to warm up before doing Kop Jarn. If you have a shoulder problem
you may need to modify the action, but the essence of it is to come
over the top and rain down upon the enemy's head and/or face.

Swing back to the other side. We note that the left hand is pulling as you execute the right elbow. This provides frightening two-way power and energy. We repeat: the left hand is not passive. Grab with it as you turn. This trains both a backward elbow strike and a powerful Lop-to-elbow strike.

Complete the Kop-Jarn action with the right elbow.

Biu Jee

Sifu Jason is slightly exaggerating the hand position so that you see clearly that the "spent shell" of the right Kop-Jarn is turned into a violent strike or grab as the left Kop-Jarn is executed.

Complete the left Kop-Jarn. It's very common to struggle with your balance as you first practice these devastating beauties. Keep working at it.

Bring the right hand under and behind the left elbow.

Execute a Biu Jee as you pull your elbow back to the center. The most common interpretation of this action is to free a pinned elbow. We respectfully disagree. On the contrary, it's to teach us to "get back at the eyes and center" after throwing such a blow as Kop-Jarn.

Bring the left hand behind the extended right.

Execute another Biu Jee as you step forward. Note that
Sifu Jason finishes this sequence "in the gap." He
performed the Kop-Jarn at 90 degrees and finishes here
at 45. There is no hard rule to this finish and you may
certainly finish this section at 90. The idea is to be able to
move professionally through a full range of motion.

Turn the palms to the top position.

Perform a double Huen-Sao (circling hand). Both hands will rotate towards the inside and circle around. Then grab as seen in the photo.

Pull back swiftly with explosive yet relaxed power.

Circle the left foot forward and over to the left side.

Once the left foot is in position, repeat with the right leg. The right will circle toward the left and then sweep outward and arc over to the right.

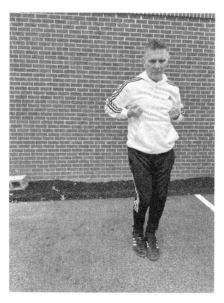

The right leg has swept toward the left. Keep your foot close to the ground as you perform the action of "Huen Ma."

The heel can't be on the ground as you do this action. Pick it up and glide on the ball of the foot. This action is the basis for takedowns, sweeps, trips, and more "creative" footwork. Many Wing Chun fighters, ill-taught, move around like they're chained to the floor. They erroneously believe that they can't "get on their toes." Once again, a false understanding of Biu Jee leads to severe application deficits. Wing Chun has amazing and fast footwork! Use it!

The return to the YJKYM. Underneath all of the "flying elbows" and circling, footwork is the foundation.

NOW REPEAT the same sequence but in reverse. This time go right, left, right, and finish on the other side.

AFTER YOU'VE FINISHED the three Kop-Jarn series on the right, we're going to do the same thing once again except we're only going to do *just one* Kop-Jarn from each side.

Just as before, execute a left Kop-Jarn with the left
elbow.

This is literally the same action as done previously. The
difference is that you're only going to do one Kop-Jarn
and then initiate the finishing sequence.

Bring the right hand under and around the left elbow.

Execute a Biu Jee as before. Sifu Jason varies the height of his eye attack when doing the form for the obvious reason that his opponent will not always be the same. Also, we again note that this can be used, as is commonly thought, as a means of freeing a trapped elbow. A completely trapped elbow, in which you're pressed against a wall, for example, is a rather extreme scenario, however. We believe that this action is best used whenever your elbow has crossed the center - whether due to your own offensive action as shown here, or because of the enemy's technique. The idea is to get back to the center-control as expeditiously as possible.

Bring the left hand under and behind the right elbow.

Step forward and execute a second Biu Jee . You might also wish to practice this as a Biu Sau defense as well. Either one is useful depending upon the circumstance.

Turn your hands over in Taan-Sao position (palm up hand).

Execute a double Huen-Sao.

Close your grip quickly using snappy power.

Pull back both arms for backward elbow strikes.

Execute a left leg circling step (Huen-Ma).

Repeat the action with your right leg.

Be smooth as you lightly sweep your right leg back to the basic stance.

Basic Yi Ji Kim Yeung Ma.

At this point repeat that same *single* Kop-Jarn sequence with the right side.

4

Section Three: Death From Above & Killer Lop Sao

Lift the hand and bring the elbow upward just like in the last section.

As before, turn completely to the right side as you execute a left Kop-Jarn. The more you practice this action the better your balance and power generation will become. This allows the Wing Chun fighter to harness great explosive power in all movements.

Unlike in the previous section, we only do one elbow rather than three. Thus, after the left Kop-Jarn bring your right hand underneath and behind the elbow. This is the same action as done in the previous section.

Execute a Biu Jee with the right hand.

Simultaneously execute a left side-palm while grabbing and using Lop-sao with the right arm. This will give you impressive power in your Lop-sao due to the torque and two-way energy. A powerful lop-sao and strike, executed properly, is a formidable infighting weapon.

Bring the arm back across the body as you turn to the facing position. The elbow should be leading the way. Be careful to maintain control of your balance throughout the movement. Practice slowly until you get the hang of it and then do it with power and speed.

Extend the Fak-sao with the left arm. Again, because of the turn it's important that your elbow lead the way so that you don't injure it during execution. This action is a sort of "two for the price of one" technique as you get a backward elbow strike AND the Fak-sao. If you focus only on the edge of the hand rather than the elbow it's likely that you'll hyper-extend the elbow when you do this action with speed, so be careful to watch your form.

With snap and power, bring your elbow back into the middle. This is the *Biu Jee Fook-sao* position. It continues the running theme of Biu Jee - that is, using maximum torque and range and then coming back to dominance of the center. Wing Chun is not a slap hitting art, but a maximum power system that doesn't sacrifice economy of motion for power, nor power for the economy of motion. Both are in play.

Many families place their right hand palm-up on the left arm's Fook-sao and then drive forward. This adds a twisting action to the technique and is a perfectly valid interpretation to add to your toolbox. Sifu Jason, however, uses it as a Wu-sao action to drive the hand forward. This is another example of Wing Chun's aggressiveness. The "lost hand" thrusts forward into the fray. Sifu Jason finds this a very common technique during infighting and wants every opportunity to practice doing it with power and speed.

Complete the two-way action by pulling the left arm back into the chambered position and thrust the right hand forward. As usual, the elbows are driving the bus, so speak. Don't focus merely on the hands.

Turn the hand over into the palm-up position.

Begin the Huen-sao (circling hand) action.

Close your fist with a snappy grab at the end of the
circling hand action.

Pull back using elbow power to execute a Lop-sao or
backward elbow strike.

Repeat this sequence from the right side…of course, everything will
be in reverse.

5

Section Four - Destruction Down Low

Do another Kop-Jarn elbow with the left.

You're only throwing one elbow in this sequence just like
the last time.

As before, place your right hand behind the elbow.

Sifu Jason thrusts his right hand forward in a Biu Jee.
It shot across the center and finished high at the
shoulder line. This can, as said previously, be used in
a variety of ways. It can be a Man-sao (asking hand),
Biu Sao (thrusting hand), or even a fak-sao. Each
action has its place. Remember: forms are structural
foundations of applications. They are not chains.

Pull the right arm back as you execute a left palm strike. This action should be done powerfully and with Yiu-ma (waist energy) too. This is done by driving the left hip forward with the palm strike. Many people, ignorant of this application option, throttle their attack off Lop-sao because they always try to strike high. But an attack to the body is highly effective when executing Lop-sao.

Execute a Fak-sao with the left arm by shifting and bringing the arm across and up through the center.

Repeat the action from the last section by pulling the elbow back into the center and executing the Biu-jee Fook-sao.

Sifu Jason places his right hand on the inner elbow of his left and prepares to use two-way energy.

With snap and power, pull the left arm back and drive the Wu-sao forward. Once again, instead of Wu-sao you may simply place the right hand palm up on the left and then execute the action. Using the Wu-sao, we believe, gives you a more direct understanding of the aggression needed to dominate a close-range life-or-death struggle.

Snap the hand over into the palm-up position. This is technically a Taan-sao (palm-up hand) in terms of the description of what the action looks like. It's not, however, a full-throttled Taan-sao, i.e., spreading hand action.

Execute the Huen-sao circling hand.

Grab powerfully.

Pull the right arm back into the chambered position as
done previously.

Of course, then repeat the exact same sequence from the right side to close out the section.

6

Section Five: Gaun Sao

The Gaun-sao is an excellent defensive tool that covers a wide swath of territory with a single action.

Take a moment in your YJKYM and take a breath. Check to see if you maintained positional integrity throughout the previous sections and, importantly, haven't gotten tense. As always, relax.

Execute a "scissors" Guan-sao as you shift to your right. The movement is powered by the Yiu Ma (waist energy). The shift is slightly to the right, not passing 45 degrees.

The high left arm hinges at the elbow as the hand tucks inward toward the inner right elbow. The right arm withdraws slightly as you lift in into the higher position. You can see these motions as large Huen-sao type actions where you're changing positions similar to the "wrestler's pummel" drill.

Use the Yiu Ma to execute another Guan-sao, this time with your right hand in the high position. The sweep of the motion is designed to cover you against all attacks to the middle and high gate.

Move your arms into position to initiate a final Guan-Sao action.

Yiu Ma again powers you into the 45 degrees "side-on stance" with a final Guan-sao action. The proper use of energy is critical so that the body and arms move as one unit. Gaun-sao is not an "arms only" action!

Execute a Lop-sao with the left hand as you draw it back into the chambered position. Simultaneously bring the right hand into the Fook-sao middle position - use a small semi-circular motion powered by the shift to bring the Fook-sao back to center.

Left hand is placed on the right arm.

Use two-direction energy to thrust the left arm forward and the right pulls back into an elbow strike. Again, some families finish with he left arm facing palm down. We prefer the Wu-sao application due to its efficacy and frequency in combat.

Begin the Huen-sao circling hand action.

Close the hand tightly so that you develop a strong, snappy grip.

Pull the left arm back sharply.

Repeat on the other side.

7

Fak Sao

The Faak-sao (neck killing hand) section is shown from the left-side only. Repeat the same actions in reverse after doing the left.

Start from the YJKYM.

Bring your left arm forward and low across the middle of your body (as seen in reverse in the next photo) and then execute a sharp Faak-sao with the left and Paak-sao with the right. Some lineages use this action as a Mann-sao (asking/inquisitive hand) and that's not wrong.
Sifu Jason executes an aggressive "neck killing hand" with the energy focused on the outside edge of the hand. As you'll also note, he has the action carry slightly past the shoulder line so as to follow through. Much like with the Kop-Jarn action, Biu Jee emphasizes great power and, as Mike Tyson would say, hitting with bad intentions.

The right hand drops out of the Paak-sao position and sweeps through the full range of motion. The left hand follows the action.

Execute the right Faak-sao and left Paak-sao.

Sweep the hands back across the body and execute the Faak-
sao/Paak-sao again.

Bring the left hand back to the center. Point to note is that you should let your left be in front of the motion back to center and then drop your hand suddenly with Jut-sao. This will help you develop power as you attack the center from an outside position. Jut-sao is a short explosive jolt/jerk on the enemy arm that's extremely useful against a stiff opponent. The right hand is pulled back sharply into the chambered fist position next to the body.

Yiu Ma is used as the left hand executes a Huen-sao. This action, when mastered, can become a dynamite action that elevates your infighting game. When in a tie-up (hand-fighting with an enemy) this non-static Huen-sao allows the skilled Wing Chun fighter to quickly change angles and position while still controlling the enemy. It's another of Wing Chun's deceptive techniques that look so harmless - even a little weird - but has vast application capacity.

Use Yiu Ma and circle the left back to the center. This is a "seed" idea that has multiple applications. For example, in practice, the Wing Chun fighter might use the "large" Huen-sao to dissipate the enemy's pressure and change angles, and then shoot back toward center with a smashing attack. A side-palm to the jaw works wonders! It's a wonderful way to scramble a dude's eggs. Herein is yet another example - a brilliant one - of how Wing Chun is a system of principles and structures limited only by our need and philosophical honesty. It's a clear case of "principled pragmatism."

Use the large Huen-sao action to the outside again.

Return to the center as before.

Execute the large Huen-sao a third time.

Return to center again.

Place the right hand on the left arm. Check and make sure that you're in the YJKYM. It's quite common that explosive shifting can cause a deterioration of our basic structure and stance.

Use two-way energy and execute a powerful Wu-sao hand back to the middle while simultaneously drawing the left arm back into an elbow strike.

Turn the hand over into the palm-up position.

Execute a Huen-sao and then powerfully close your fist.
Once again, grip strength is an essential quality in life and
in combat.

Draw the right arm back with power.

Repeat from the right side to complete the section.

8

Long Range Destruction

Start from the YJKYM as usual (not pictured). Bring the
left hand in to the center.

Execute a left Biu-Jee attack. Use snappy energy with the technique and have your fingers extended and thumb tucked in as shown.

Place your right underneath the left elbow.

Execute a fast Biu-Jee attack.

Fire another fast Biu-Jee with the left and at the finish,
draw the right hand back into the chambered position.
The timing of the strikes should be one…two, three. In
other words, throw the first, pause slightly, and then throw
the next two in quick succession.

Turn to the right and execute a heavy strike with the palm to the neck/jaw level. The side-palm strike to the jaw is a devastating weapon that takes the life out of people. It's like having a girl say, "you're such a good friend." It's like that. Nasty.

Like before, sweep the left across the body, low to high, and execute a powerful Faak-sao using the edge of the hand.

Drive the elbow back into center and drop the elbow downward in Jut-sao. This action is hard to show in a photo sequence so think of the return to center as two distinct actions here. It will return to the center and then Jut down as the elbow and wrist pull downward slightly. During infighting, the Jut-Sao is a devastating technique to use against a stiff opponent who is unskilled in the ways of proper energy use. It takes advantage of the fact that stiffness leaves one unable to quickly adjust to pulls and changes of direction.

Place the right arm on the inside of the left elbow just like you did in the previous sections.

Using two-way energy, thrust the right forward and pull the left arm back into the chambered position.

Turn the palm over into the palm-up position.

Just as before, execute a Huen-Sao, close the fist (not pictured but shown in previous sections) and then pull back.

Finish in the Yi Ji Kim Yueng Ma.

Repeat this on the other side now, beginning with the right hand Biu-Jee and finishing with the left arm. The thing to remember through all of this is that the heart and soul of the *Thrusting Fingers* form is that no matter the chaos of a fight, we seek the simplest means of survival. And at a distance that is, indubitably, fast and consecutive eye spears/jabs as practiced here. Don't overlook this section (or any for that matter, but especially this one) as though it's doing something you already know. In point of fact, it's teaching us to fire eye strikes from a distance *IN COMBINATION*. To do that requires *relaxed aggression*, which is the very thing Biu Jee helps us understand and practice. To throw these devastating beauties in blistering combinations, while on the move, with broken rhythm, greatly extends one's reach in a fight *AND* their stopping power.

9

Chin Na - Seize & Control

Start the section as usual in the Yi Ji Kim Yueng Ma. At this level of you may still experience some difficulty in seamlessly getting back to your "neutral" position due to all the power/energy you're putting into the technique. This can be expected and you'll get better with practice. Just make sure to "find" your YJKYM every time and you'll do fine.

Turn the hands over and then thrust the elbows forward
as you execute a snappy, powerful double-hand grab.

Grip powerfully after the jolting action. This will give you
considerable power and control of the enemy.

Both hands then execute a Lop-Sao across the body. Sifu Jason pulls slightly down and his left elbow moves in line with the left hip to add more power to the Yiu-Ma action. The traditional set keeps the turning grab at shoulder height. By bringing one's hands lower, though, the Wing Chun fighter is better able to use this double-hand Lop-Sao to pull the enemy off balance by virtue of the simultaneous pull and lowering of the center of gravity. Furthermore, the lower pulling action allows for more use of the hip power. The higher the arms (in the traditional action) is weaker because it's less dependent upon the waist and more upon the deltoids.

Sifu Jason returns with a left hooking punch. The idea isn't that it's a hook or uppercut but that we use an arcing half-circle offensive action. The critical thing is to use logic with our fighting and not mindlessly limit ourselves to thinking, "oh, Wing Chun doesn't use this or that…the hook is boxing, so we don't use it." On the contrary, Wing Chun uses the whole body *logically* for the goal of defending and attacking.

In this section we don't bring the other hand into play. We just execute the closing sequence with the same hand.

Execute the Huen-Sao and then close the fist strongly.

Pull back with power...so much that you create a ripple in
the time-space continuum and Marty McFly can't get
back to the future. Okay...maybe not that much, but you
get the idea.

Repeat with the other side, using the same double hand Lop-Sao
grab action but go right instead of left. This grab and control is a
doorway into Wing Chun's great diversity of application. In this
case, it implies the art of Chin-Na, or Chinese grappling. That is to
say, to seize and control the enemy. By learning to grab, push, pull,
and throw - and adding this to your already existing striking skill -
you become a very well-rounded fighter. It's a mistake to think of
Wing Chun as merely a striking system although many fall into that
fallacy...trying to chain-punch everything that isn't nailed down. In
fact, Wing Chun fundamentals offer us a logical diet of seize and
control techniques and tactics. A full exploration of them is beyond
the scope of this volume and we'll cover them, God willing, in a
volume to come down the road.

10

Saam Bai Fut...the Big Splash

We again start from the YJKYM. But this time we do the completely unexpected! For all of Wing Chun's emphasis upon economy of motion and centerline, suddenly we're bending at the waist and thrusting our hands toward the floor.

Cover your head as you begin to stand back up. This is a critical skill to practice and apply should you ever hit the ground in a fight and have to stand back up. PROTECT YOUR HEAD!

Okay…more craziness! Throw your hands over your head and circle them backward and then bring them back to center.

What's this all about? Glad you asked! You're in a fight. Never forget that. Perhaps the greatest single piece of genius in all of Wing Chun is found right here. Seriously. In combat, when all you-know-what has broken loose, you must do what you need to in order to survive. Don't worry about the rules if the rules get in your way because the main rule - the BIG one - is to survive. In other words, the idea here isn't to specifically apply this action so much as it is to adapt to the immediate reality. Wing Chun proves itself in this to be a self-defense science. How? By conceding that a situation might very well arise that you were unprepared for - and that your training didn't equip you to answer. Expect the unexpected and do what you need to do. Survive. Wing Chun didn't die for you, so don't die for it. Use it! Don't be used by it!

Drop back down again. We actually practice falling in our school. Not just break falls but how to collapse into a defensible position and still fight. This, we believe, is in the spirit of Saam Bai Fut.

Come back up while covering your noggin. We have to prioritize things and our brain is more important than our ribs if we're forced to choose .

Execute the big splash (as we jokingly call it here) once you come back up. Some families swing their arms forward, then back. You can do that if you want. You can flap your arms like a big, crazy bird for all we care. That's not the point. We think the main idea is to remind us that a fight isn't going to be a movie scene and we must be gritty and prepared to adapt. Do what needs to be done.

Back to our recognizable position. Adaptability doesn't
mean we jettison the basics, only that we're prepared to
do what's necessary in order to get back to them.

Third time down to show the importance of the concept.

Covering the head again.

Wave the arms back and then bring them to the center
one last time.

Back to the primary position.

Right punch.

Left punch. See…we're back to our fundamentals. Exceptions like this section don't destroy the rules. Rather, they reinforce them. An exception is exactly that which proves the logic of the rule. (And for you philosophy/theology geeks out there: such is a wondrous window through which we peer out into that great and wide vastness of the one-and-the-many… that is, we catch glimpse of life's unity AND diversity.) This part of Biu Jee is the physical manifestation of the principle of adaptability. Many Wing Chun *fundamentalists* obsess about technical details. They say things like, "you can't do that in Wing Chun." They miss this exigent point. Adapt and survive. Use the fundamentals; don't be bound to them. Or, "learn the principle, abide by the principle, dissolve the principle."

Right punch. One way of seeing this concept is to imagine escaping from a takedown and mount…and then getting back your feet…and the fundamentals.

The left punch again.

The fifth and final punch in the closing sequence.

Initiate the closing sequence of palm-up hand with the right.

Execute a Huen-Sao.

Grab powerfully and close your hand.

Pull back into the chambered position and you're all set.

Sifu Jason slides his left foot to his right in order to finish. Some families use their right. It's not a hill to die on. Use either one. It's not like figure skating. You don't need to stick the landing. Congrats. You're all done. Go have a cookie to celebrate.

11

Applications

The thing to remember about fights and fighting is that it's going to be chaotic. This should go without saying, right? It's like reminding you that when you go to the beach that the water is wet. Or that your ex was crazy. Yeah…it seems like that, but it bears repeating due to the ego of man *and* the love we have of our toys. Wing Chun can become an ego trip if we aren't careful. We can love the acquisition of its knowledge and forget that its use is something needed in the worst possible way. Also, lots of us dudes have a love of our toys. For example, I love my truck (Toyota Tundra). Trucks are cool. Epically cool, in my opinion. Some guys like a sports car. That's all fine. But my point is that we can get a little too in love with the mechanics of the system and forget that Wing Chun is going to be used in a violent mash-up event, not a nice and cordial, or sanctioned event. Now, granted, a sporting event like boxing or MMA, is violent enough and the anxiety before a match is legendary. That's true. But the reality of a self-defense situation is like that - but on steroids - because there's usually anger and shock involved.

Anger because the person attacking you is usually, for whatever reason, enraged.

Shock because we often can't believe that "this is happening."

It's for this reason that we should soberly and humbly submit to the lessons of the system. The first two forms provided for us the foundation structure we're using. The primary drills like Chi-Sao give us the unique ability to function dynamically with that structure. But fighting is fighting and we must resist with every fibre of our being the temptation to try and look good in a fight. If we've been diligent in our training, the structure is there and will be used as needed. But if we try and impose a version of what we think Wing Chun ought to look like on the fight, then we're in serious danger. Don't ever worry about what it looks like. Survive. Shut down the enemy's attack and either escape or demolish his functional capacity so that he's no longer a threat to your safety. That's the only thing that matters when you're in a true fight. Anyone that stays on the sidelines crying and moaning about your technique being sloppy is the worst of the worst type of critic. What they're truly saying is that your life and safety must be defended according to their personal and completely arbitrary standards.

Nonsense! Balderdash! Rubbish!

Biu Jee isn't "violating" the center line in the form with all the elbows and elaborate motions. On the contrary, it's teaching us that through the training in the rest of the system *that you have gained skill in the fundamentals and will use those fundamentals accordingly without being bound by them.*

In the next series of application photos you'll see Glenn attacking me in a cramped room. It isn't a ring or cage and there are no timers, refs, safe footing, or anything else. The toughest part about self-defense fighting is that we very often don't know when it starts. It's the bad guy that gets the privilege of saying "go." This means that we're often in some kind of ambush-style attack, which is a serious bit of business. We need to be ready for that, body, mind and soul. That initial onslaught is going to be swift. It's going to be shockingly aggressive. So, be ready. Don't lie to yourself about having a perfect Taan-Sao and all that. Trust your training and get down to business. Your only focus is shutting down the attack and either getting out of the danger zone or eradicating the threat entirely.

That's "perfect" Wing Chun. And that's what Biu Jee is telling us. Look good doing your forms. In a fight, get it done! Be swift. Be smart. Be nasty. Eye jabs/gouges. Elbows. Groin hits. Head butts. Knees. Whatever it takes…because your life and safety are no one else's business.

INTERCEPTION

Of course, you can always just eye jab a dude before the fight ever starts. Just in case. The problem with this is that if's not exactly legal…so there's that. But seriously, in this case I launched right as I thought my enemy was going to throw a punch. This is a subject unto itself but suffice it to say that if you have reason to fear an attack is imminent, and evasiveness or escape are impossible, you don't have to wait for the enemy to launch. This presupposes that you're not doing something immoral or illegal in the first place. As always, living according to the moral law of God makes straight your path and provides clarity. Stay out of other people's business, treat them with respect always, don't trespass, and try to deescalate. If these fail, an interception might be in order. The eye attack used here, long, vicious, and so very fast, should be used at every opportunity. Learn to throw it like an Ali-jab…in combination and on the move. Again: at distance, these long eye-jabs are utterly devastating. Practice them until you're so fast and accurate that you have to think about them to do them wrong.

DEFENSE & COUNTER

In this case, Glenn launches a right hand swing. Since I'm in a cramped corner, I use a simultaneous Biu Sao to catch the punch and a right elbow.

In this case I couldn't achieve a Lin Siu Daai Da (simultaneous attack and defense). But notice that I'm set up for a counterattack with either an elbow or an eye attack. Notice also that I'm in a slight crouch. It's a tremendous mistake to leave your head up when dealing with an ambush. Protect your head and chin! On the inside, stay small. Stay low.

SCISSORS GAUN SAO

A "scissors" Gaun-Sao can be helpful too. Personally I prefer the previous defense, but some people like the sweeping coverage they get from the Gaun-Sao. It leaves you exposed to the next attack from the other side, so you must be prepared to shift back in a hurry. Again, I'm not fond of it personally, but I'm not the one fighting for you. You are. If you can make it work, have at it.

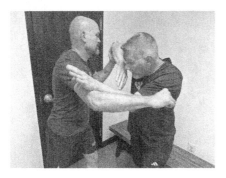

In this instance after the Gaun, I swing back to pick up the next strike with the Biu Sao guard and quickly counter attack. Notice the angle of my Biu Sao. It's thrusting straight into the line of Glenn's punch, thereby cutting it off.

This time I use the scissors the other way. Notice again that I have my head down and I'm ready to crash forward to cut off Glenn's ambush. It's a still photo and that can make us over-daring. In reality, Glenn is firing hard and fast and I've got to be prepared to cut him off since I have very limited space.

I get right back to the attack by shifting into his center with a guard hand and an elbow strike. This "two-for-one" is what we're always looking for if we can achieve it. Offense and defense all in one!

SURPRISE ATTACK FROM THE SIDE

Glenn, playing the nefarious bad guy, attacks from the side this time. This often happens in a multiple opponent scenario where another fighter enters the fray after the fight starts. It's for this reason that Wing Chun includes techniques that cover the flank. It's not all center line, guys! It's more than simply chain punching and Chi-Sao. To deal with this, I execute a whipping hand (Faak-Sao) and Paak-Sao, as seen in the form. The adjustment I make is trying to hide my head and swaying a little to absorb the incoming blow.

A best case scenario is that the Faak-Sao nails Glenn in the neck or throat and then I can safely turn and finish him. Sometimes you "miss" and your forearm smashes him in the face. This is the thing with an all-out ambush and exactly why we have techniques like Faak-Sao!

SURPRISE ATTACK FROM BEHIND

I play the bad guy now. Perhaps I hate bald people because they remind me of Lex Luthor. Whatever the case, I attack from behind and Glenn turns with a reverse elbow, which is done in the form every time you turn from one Kop Jarn to another.

Once he turns, he's in position to continue his counterattack. Doing this requires quite a bit of balance, incidentally. Wing Chun addresses this, and prepares us, with the turning step back in the Chum Kiu form, and the extreme shifting of the Kop Jarn in Biu Jee. Keeping one's balance in all-out fighting is a critical sklll and precisely why we need to do the forms so much. Remember, develop the correct structural foundation through the forms, drill the correct muscle memory with the drills, and then be free to apply these in all-out and unpredictable combat. This is the correct integration of structure (forms), fluidity (drills), and application (tactics). Mistakes abound when we play one aspect over against the other. Each aspect is important and connected to the others.

SURPRISE ATTACK WHILE SEATED

Though the Wing Chun master should be quite savvy to the schemes of immoral men and not leave themselves in such a vulnerable position when violence beckons, we nevertheless need to consider defense in all scenarios. Covering up is better than just getting pummeled but not by much in some cases. Without boxing gloves on it's hard to use an effective cover.

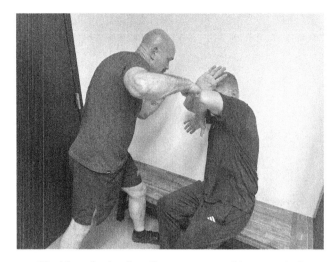

The idea of using the elbows as a guard is suggested throughout Biu Jee. We can also use the forearms but this "weaponizes" the defense in the event that Glenn punches my elbow, in which case he's likely to break his paw.

Of course, he might not hit my elbow. Things are chaotic. That's why my left hand is in a guard position too and my head is down. Always protect your head! That's the point of Saam Bai Fut. Also, you can't see it but I'm doing my hearty best to peer out through the gap in my arms to see what Glenn is doing. We must train to keep our eyes open at all times or else we're fighting the invisible man by default.

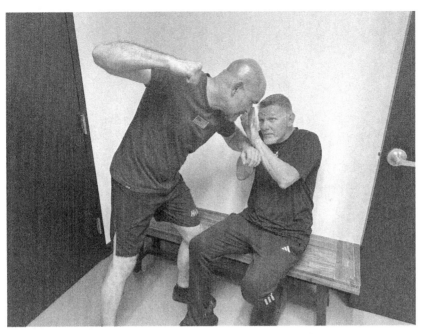

In the middle of a barrage there's likely to be an opportunity for counter attack, so we much keep our eyes open and be ready to seize the opportunity even in the midst of the storm. In this case I look to hit his eyes because he brought his head close. It's very important to consider one of the misapprehensions of Biu Jee again here. Many lineages teach that we throw the darting eye jab from under/behind the Kop Jarn because our elbow has been pushed and pinned by the opponent. That's certainly acceptable but we think it's hardly the ONLY use, nor the main one, of the action. On the contrary, Biu Jee teaches us that no matter where we are in the chaos of combat to seek out the eye attack since there's so much "bang for our buck" in them.

The earlier we recognize the threat, the better. In this case I've been able to identify the incoming threat and have a slight window of opportunity. Of course, in a still photo it looks like I have time/space to stand up, but that's wishful thinking. Glenn is moving in too fast. Never underestimate how quick and vicious an assault is in real life. This is why we must develop simple actions for use. Complexity always breaks down under the heavy pressure of a violent assault. I don't want to rush. If I stand up before I have control I might very well get pushed over and end up in an even worse position. Staying seated, therefore, may very well be your best defensive position until you have a clear opening to get up. This is another example, albeit a strange one, of the core Wing Chun concept of "fighting from the bridge" and Chui Ying/Bi Ying. In other words, always endeavor to fight from superior position. If you don't have one, stalemate until you can. In other words, *build a bridge; never fight across the stream!*

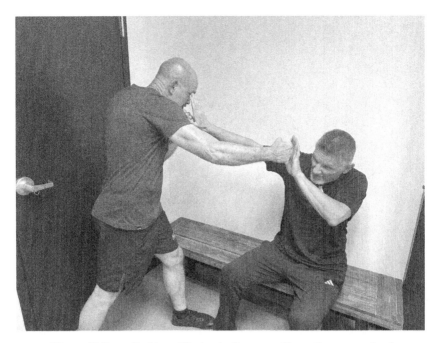

If I can, I'll throw that long Biu Jee to the eyes. It's another example of how important it is to practice our eye attacks from a variety of angles and, in this case, positions. From a seated position it's virtually impossible to throw a significant strike that has enough payload to stop an attacker. Meanwhile, he (the opponent) has all the leverage. This being the case, the Biu Jee form encourages us to use wisdom. Stay covered and get skillful at eye attacks. All-out fights won't always find us at our best, so we must have the ability to react skillfully even under the worst types of pressure.

SOME EXTRA POINTS ON THE ISSUE

A significant error in Wing Chun is the assumption of contact points. Bridging and clinching are an art unto themselves. Because the enemy isn't cooperating, nor a Wing Chun fighter himself, the types of tie-ups and reactions we'll see are going to be different than in class. Chi-Sao training is essential for "energy sensitivity" and structural/reflexive skill for the Wing Chun fighter. That's true. But it can also develop a "Chi-Sao monster" who can murder people at the drill but can't fight with the attributes the drill is supposed to have developed in the first place. Both are important but many students and schools are either-or. We should have skillful Chi-Sao **and** clinch fighting.

Modern infighters are better than ever due to the advent of BJJ and MMA. Short eye attacks and elbows are an absolute **must have** against effective infighters of our era. One of the big ideas in Biu Jee is to learn to deliver eye attacks and elbows with great rapidity. Never expect to end the fight with any single blow! Always think combinations! Chain punching is a core skill that should inform our use of other techniques. Imagine throwing an elbow-eye jab-elbow with the same speed you'd throw a chain punch!!

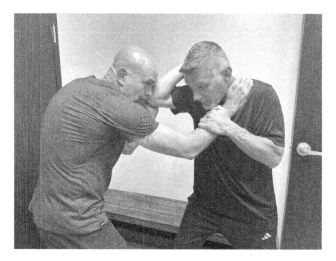

Though not shown directly in the Biu Jee form, the upward elbow is implied. It's a devastating weapon in close. The actions, as always, should be quick and snappy. Avoid being tense. Speed and control are key. In this case, Sifu Jason uses a quick upward elbow to take advantage of a short opening after the eye jab.

He follows up with another elbow from the other side. Elbows for attack and defense are critical skills to master for contemporary infighting. The chain punch is, surprising as it is to hear, **virtually useless** during such close-quarter fighting because both hands are needed - one for attack and the other for control. Disengaging to throw a series of punches is foolhardy. The chain punch is a finishing move but the elbows, short hooks (especially to the body), and eye attacks are workhorses during bridge/clinch fighting.

Ah! But it can go both ways. Control is the key. Just striking without having the skill of control can easily lead you into an exchange. If you can do it, so can he. Don't forget that. Control is first. Always. Never sacrifice defense (control) for offense.

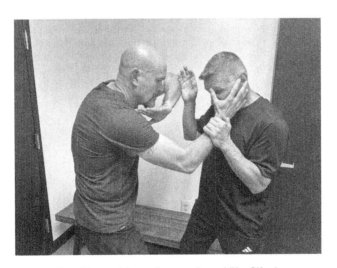

Not that this would ever happen in real life. Sifu Jason is indomitable. Chuck Norris checks under his bed for Sifu Jason. Seriously. We're just showing this to remind you lesser boys and girls out there to stay in contact-control during infighting.

The thumb to the eye is a brutal part of infighting, so use it at every opportunity. It's the glaring weakness of sport based combat systems but we mustn't get overconfident. If you can't handle the pressure of the clinch (grappling and hand-fighting), you'll find it nearly impossible to achieve success. Proper Chi-Sao training should produce skill at this range ESPECIALLY against non-Wing Chun fighters like grapplers and Muay Thai stylists.

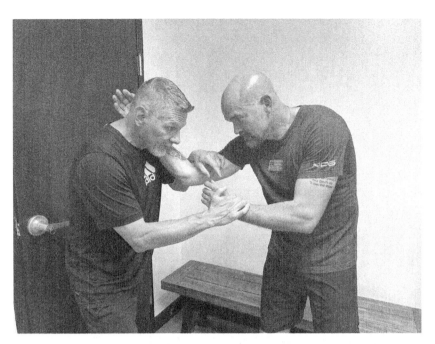

Here Glenn and I are in a struggle for control. A point to commit to heart is that infighting is about control first and striking (or anything else) second. The idea of Chi-Sao is to teach us skillful control on the inside without contradiction. We seek to become masters of attacking the weakest targets while simultaneously controlling their balance and shutting down their offense. But this doesn't mean we disregard alternate approaches just because they don't attack the eyes and throat like we do . The neck-tie, as Glenn is using, is a very common tactic and one we must get good at using and defending. Many Wing Chun schools ignore the skill of Muay Thai fighters or wrestlers because of snobbery. The thing to know is that Wing Chun is more scientific and realistic overall than those systems but that doesn't mean they're completely ineffective. In fact, due to the fact that they train against resistance all the time, they often have an edge against the Wing Chun exponent who only does forms and "polite" Chi-Sao with too many restrictions.

MORE PROBLEMS TO CONSIDER...AND SOLVE

Beth finds herself on the ground. Now, in order to cover Wing Chun's application to ground fighting will require another volume altogether. But suffice it say here that the system gives us the principles to apply to any particular situation (by process of deduction...that is, reasoning from the general to the particular). In this case, Beth assumes a good defensive position. Her hands are up and she's ready to move/scoot or scramble as needed.

Realizing that Rob has the burden of the attack, Beth waits and uses a basic upward kick as he comes into range.

For a female especially, the ground position has certain advantages if we know how to use them. By using a sort-of fence guard, Beth is able to keep her powerful legs in play. In this case, Rob catches a kick in the nethers. Poor fella. The knee and groin are pretty good targets for Beth and if you have shoes/sneakers on it's even better. (Another reason to wear smart footwear). Practice moving and scooting from the ground position and learn to kick quickly and with power from your back. There are some who decry any fighting off the back (or all ground fighting). They insist that there's no ground fighting in Wing Chun. The problem is that they're missing a key concept of Biu Jee (that survival often requires adaptation). What should we do if we get taken down? What happens if we trip, or get knocked down? Give up? Just die?! Traditionalism is contradictory because it places the past above the goal of the system, which is survival. Wing Chun is a true combat art and science since it gives us BOTH the logic of structure AND the freedom to adapt to unforeseen circumstances.

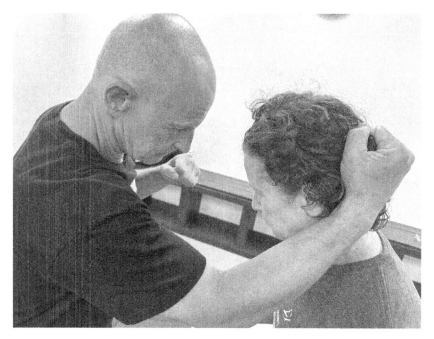

A common challenge for women is a hair-grab. A ponytail is a handle for a bad guy. A good defense for this is to move forward quickly and execute a head butt to the face if you can. This works in the clinch quite well, incidentally, and not only against a hair grab. But a head butt isn't a "head smash" as seen in movies. Rather, it's a quick jab to the face with the top of one's head. Doing so makes life rather uncomfortable for the bad guy, like a holiday at the in-laws. In some cases, a good head butt can end a fight. The movies have given us the impression that it hardly works but that's crazy. In real life a good head butt is nasty business. There are, again, those who say that you can't head butt in Wing Chun. This type of thinking exposes the idolatry at the heart of traditionalism. There are no "sinful" tactics and techniques; only more or less efficient tools. To say that we can't do something implies, by virtue of the prohibition, that it's immoral. That's ridiculous in the extreme. The head butt is implied in the ducking action in the form's last section. We're just talking about freedom of application. A Paak-da (paak-sao and punch) aren't shown directly in the forms either, but no one doubts that it's part of Wing Chun. As the great Wong Shun Leung said, "don't be Wing Chun's slave, make it your slave."

Beth follows up (or leads..always think in combination) with an upward whack to Rob's groin. If someone has control of your head, get low and attack the groin.

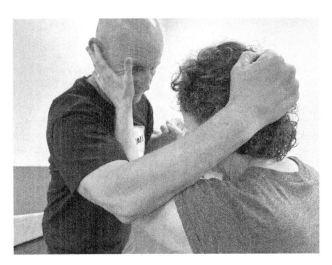

Again in combination, Beth takes advantage of the opening and thumbs Rob in the eye.

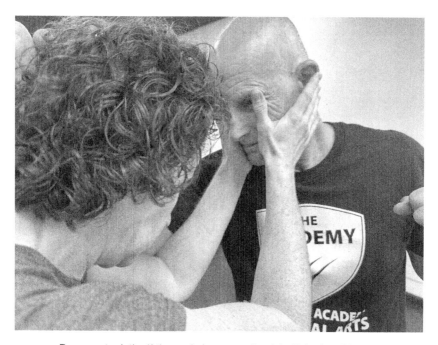

Be opportunistic. If the groin is open, whack it. If the head butt is there, take it. Or attack the eyes. It's not one movement and that's the end of it. You may try one and end up, by virtue of the other guy reacting, getting the other. Let us not forget that if we're in a fight with a deranged opponent, one intent on killing us (or rape and then murder for that matter), who may or may not be on drugs, attacking soft targets may be our only way to survive. Proper training - physically and emotionally - is key. Beth is ready to go all-in. She's ready to do whatever it takes to win/survive. Going half-heartedly after the eyes, groin, or throat is a sure way to lose! We should be twice as skillful and just as mean, if not more so, than the most rabid aggressor. King David didn't have PTSD after killing Goliath. Living by the right moral code and treating others respectfully while obeying property laws is the key to knowing when you need to fight. And if forced to go, really go! Failure is horrific. A half-hearted counterattack is worse than no counterattack. Beth's intent is to totally stop Rob's immoral assault by any means necessary.

Don't try a head butt if you can't secure the line. Don't go "head to head". And don't use your forehead either - use only the top of your head and only to his face. In this case, Rob has such a snug clinch on Beth that she can't get a good line. But don't panic. You may have to struggle for a bit but keep your cool and your balance - even if you get thrown around a bit (another situation where Wing Chun footwork is made for the real world). In sport fighting there are weight classes but in real life you may end up facing someone who has the strength to shove you all over the place. Wing Chun's YJKYM, properly understood and trained, provides the basis for "pushed" and "pulled" footwork. Likely developed by a women, this makes sense.

By having solid but springy structure, and tie-up footwork, Beth is able to get a moment of advantage and uses it to deliver a sharp knee to the groin.

If you miss with the groin attack it's often because the enemy threw his hips back in defense. This generally opens him to a follow-up knee to the midsection. Sometimes even the head. Remember: think in combination.

Beth can follow up with a short knee to the groin after missing one to the head or midsection. Or after a missed strike of some sort in which she transitions to a clinch. Don't forget that a smaller person like Beth (compared to Rob in this case anyway) can initiate infighting in order to deliver powerful blows like this one. Though the knee isn't thrown in the Biu Jee form, it's implied through the use of the elbow. Plus, it can be seen as a "half-way" kick when one throws the basic kick in Chum Kiu.

Though already referenced, it bears repeating that a larger opponent can very readily rain down blows upon you. In this case, Beth uses the cross-arm guard to try and break Rob's hands.

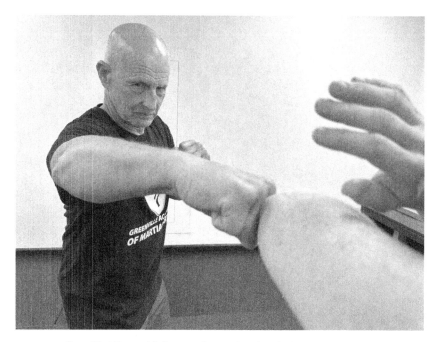

Do mitt drills and light sparring to develop timing and distance control. Don't just stand there and hope the guy is stupid and will just hit you on the elbow. Once you get skillful at using this guard you'll have a good answer to overhands and hooks that taller foes can threaten you with. As always, think in totality - in combination - not just one thing. This is part of your overall arsenal, so be ready to use it and then make adjustments as needed.

As Sadie smashes Rob AND defends his punch simultaneously, we just want to remind you that Wing Chun, being a fistic science (and art), takes into serious consideration the reality of size differential. For this reason, Wing Chun is a type of guerrilla style fighting. Superior strength and body mass give one significant advantages in a fight and to mitigate against them the Wing Chun fighters must develop both a high level of evasive, yet aggressive, footwork, and blitzkrieg style attacks.

Though she's smaller than Rob, Sadie works on tying him up when she needs to. Jim Driscoll, the former boxing great that influenced Bruce Lee and his Jeet Kune Do, wrote that the clinch is part of footwork. Get that? We can't outmaneuver everyone. A good "bridge" (clinch) game is an absolute must. Often, a smaller person eschews this aspect of fighting because they erroneously think that they can't excel at close range. But this is the whole point. Sadie is working on shutting down Rob's attack and quickly launching her own. The idea is control and speed…both, not one or the other.

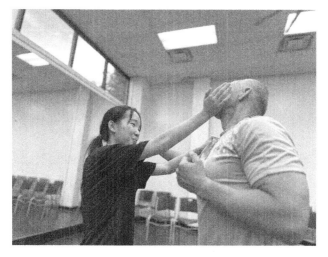

With proper training, Wing Chun allows Sadie to control and attack with consummate skill. Soft targets like the eyes, jaw, neck, throat and groin are always in play and help shorten the gap of strength she has with Rob.

Sadie, being small, is often pitted against people literally twice her bodyweight. Here she's working on evasiveness, parrying, and bridging with David. Notice her high guard. It's suicide for her to go out there and keep both hands extended in front against a taller and stronger opponent who has the ability to reach around that extended guard with power.

What can't be conveyed in a photo is Sadie's swift footwork. By using angles and tactical movement - and timing! - she catches David in between movements…in pursuit. She cuts him off (intercepts him, that is) with a bridging action.

Quickly, she launches a knee. Notice David's high guard. This is the type of thing you'll likely encounter from today's fighters and it's exactly why Sadie bridged and then launched a low-line attack.

In this case, Rob gets a hold of Glenn. There are numerous "bridge" points that one learns to train and achieve. It's from this bridge that skillful infighters do their best work.

A common error is to attack without first building a strong bridge and this leads us into trading...or worse. Here, Rob takes advantage of Glenn's mistake and attacks while controlling him. He's not trading! He's attacking from a strong bridge.

Evasiveness and cover go hand in hand. We must learn to pick up common (and high intensity) attacks in a skillful manner. Here, Glenn's footwork has put him in position to catch Rob's right-hand swing. By angling off line he (Glenn) gave himself an extra advantage and forced Rob to "chase." This skill is essential to infighting success and takes that rare combination of patience and aggression.

Glenn's first order of business is controlling Rob's balance and shutting down his offense. To launch an attack too soon is foolhardy. Again: never sacrifice your defense for your offense.

Once Rob has made a mistake Glenn captures his head with a neck pulling hand and launches a punch at the same time. The force of this two-way energy attack is considerable. It also allows the Wing Chun fighter to punch with safety - both for their knuckles, since they've isolated the target - and for their overall defense, since they control the enemy's balance.

Punches and elbows both need to be honed for infighting. But again, notice that Glenn is controlling with one hand and striking with the other. A very common oversight when working the forms is the two-way action at their heart. For example, when throwing a Kop-jarn with one arm, don't lose focus on the "passive" arm. It's not passive at all, but active in pulling. Holding and hitting is an art form unto itself. It's the heart-and-soul of good infighting and, therefore, a skill that Wing Chun takes seriously. There's no better way to attack successfully than by holding and hitting. Grapplers use the "holding" aspect all the time in order to smother the striking ability of good boxers and kickboxers. All "advanced" Academy drills are essentially holding-and-hitting drills after gaining bridge! That's the Academy doctrine in a nutshell…bridge successfully, and then simultaneously control his balance through pushing-pulling and hit him. With everything you've got - elbows, knees, your fist, fingers, head, feet. If you lose control, angle offline and repeat.

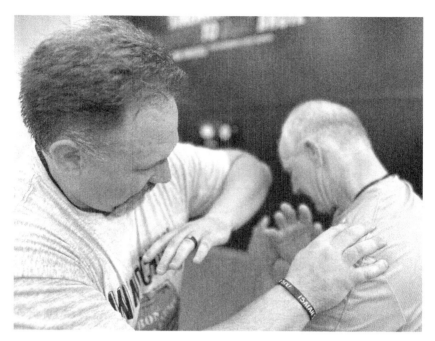

Though it seems like everyone is always beating the bejabbers out of Rob, have no worry. He's simply always the one who volunteers for the abuse. We suspect that he has brain damage now but don't want to say anything. Anyway, Jason Fort shows another type of "clinch control" here. Being a pretty big guy, Jason uses a high fence/guard, footwork, and his size to bridge with opponents. With good technique/structure combined with his imposing strength, he uses lots of shoving and pulling to gain control of his opponent. Here he's pushed Rob back and by simply having a hand on Rob's shoulder, he has "sensitivity" and control. He fires a quick and compact elbow from the control position. The skill of Wing Chun is to use the Faan-sao principle (repeating hand…combination attacking) with the other elements like pushing, pulling, and clinching. We can't say this enough: the straight blast is a PRINCIPLE of repeating hand and not merely a technique. Think of using ALL of your weapons with the rapidity of a chain punch.

Again, due to Jason's size and strength, he often has people ducking for cover and trying to outmaneuver him. He takes advantage of this with skillful footwork, pushes, pulls, and head-control as seen here. With Rob pushed off balance, Jason fires a knee to the lower body. Obviously, the body type of big Jason Fort (yes, that's literally his last name) and Beth or Sadie are different. But all of them, once they've learned the Wing Chun systematic, through drills and and Chi-sao, discover the best way to utilize their tools. Remember: skill of use requires wisdom and experience. Forms and lots of drills are one's path of getting to this level. Just knowing the form won't do it. We must drill, drill, drill in order to "find out who we are." Wing Chun won't fight for us.

David is demonstrating a powerful variation of the Kop-Jarn elbow: the overhand punch. Many Wing Chun people limit themselves to chain punches by an illogical definition of the systematic. The forms are (again!) structural foundations of applications. They aren't the fighting system themselves but foundations of it. Use what you need, when you need it. Use Wing Chun; don't be used by it.

In this photo, I catch David with an overhand. It's a mid-range tool that can catch someone really off-guard due to its angle AND the fact that the puncher's head is moving down and away from the blow. Develop this nifty shot and you can routinely catch taller fighter's over the top.

Notice the structure of the Kop-jarn "informing" the overhand punch.

Don't forget through all of this to keep the right distance. A very dangerous error is following your opponent and assuming that there's nothing he/she can do to counter your completely awesome awesomeness. There's always a counter to everything. The key is to develop good footwork and bridging skills. Here, Seanna is working on light sparring where she's moving, parrying, and clinching. It's all about control!

12

Eye-Gouges or Defense? Both

"What is it?"

Instead of looking at the structures provided in the forms and asking that question, we're better served to inquire as to what all the motion(s) can be used to accomplish.

This is certainly the case with the opening section where we have clear application ability insofar as whipping, raking, poking, and slashing at the eyes are concerned. With the weird wiggling action of the fingers (at least, that's what they look like to the average Joe or Joe-ette) it's as if our Wing Chun ancestors are saying, *"Look, stupid, there's more than one way to injure the nefarious dude's eye."*

And so there are.

From a tie-up or clinch it behooves us to have "cash in our pocket" so to say. A million and one ways of attacking the eyes is like having lots of money as far a combat is concerned. What it means is that to one with such a skill, the confrontation is always a split-second from ending. The eyes are to combat what cash is to a business - without them, we're in serious trouble. Imagine a politician trying his demagoguery and hose-job on an audience well trained in philosophy and logic. He's got nothing. Thomas Sowell remarked once (and wonderfully) that the first law of economics is scarcity and the first law of politics is to ignore the first law of economics. Likewise, the first law of all-out combat is to attack the weakest target and the first rule, it seems, of modern combat systems is to ignore this law. A country that's over $30 trillion in debt, and yet thinks it's wealthy, is bound to forget other important fundamentals too…like how to attack and defend the body's weakest targets in self-defense.

The suppression of the obvious, it appears, is mankind's greatest skill.

To this end, it's rather apropos that Wing Chun's third form makes such a show of it. *"Hey, stupid…the eyes! Kill the eyes!"* You see, as the Bible says, "there's a way that seems right to a man but its end is death." God, the Divine psychiatrist, if you will, defines us as master level truth suppressors. We're all in some way shape or form black belts in denying the obvious. Biu Jee takes that into serious consideration by reminding us of the necessity of poking the criminal dude in the eye.

I've tied-up CW and then executed a Biu Jee to the eye. Notice that the angle of the Biu Jee is upward due to the contact points. This is why I've taken to executing the Biu Jee in a slightly upward manner at some points during the form (as pictured previously).

So, what of the other version? Glad you asked.

You see, here we bump into the "one and the many" aspect of reality.

Besides jabbing, raking, slashing, gouging, and jabbing the eyes, there's also the version of Biu Jee's opening wherein the we focus on using the extended arm defensively. Instead of simultaneous attack and defense, we may find that under combat pressure that there's a need for one hand/arm to act defensively in order to cover rapid attacks raining down upon us. This is sometimes not just helpful, but downright necessary due to the fact that an enemy who's taller and/or faster is capable of unleashing a blistering assault. A Taan-da or Paak-da, though preferred, or a stop-hit for that matter, is just inaccessible in that moment. Using the extended guard to cover multiple lines works better due to the efficiency of the action; it requires less movement, which makes us functionally faster (read that: by virtue of economical technique/tactics "fast enough" to fit in with what's happening).

So, which version should we train?

Yes.

Once again we're forced to confront the apparent contradiction of Wing Chun. But it's only a contradiction for those who are looking for "*the* way" rather than "*a* way" to get things done. The first (*the way*) is a theological issue; an idol. The second (*a way*) is a logically accurate systematic meant to deal with a diversified reality that isn't going to do exactly what we want. Biu Jee is perplexing for those of us who want to put reality in a box.

Both approaches have merit insofar as combat application is concerned, so we pause to point out that this section is an excellent example of how Wing Chun isn't a fighting style per se, but rather a combat systematic meant to provide us with foundational structures and principles. How we apply them is not set in stone. Much error comes from confusing physics (centerline, balance, etc.) with tactical application. It's a categorical fallacy. Physics tells us what something is and what it does and/or doesn't do; tactics study how to use those things smartly.

In Thomas Sowell's *Intellectuals* he wisely points out the lack of wisdom of brilliant people. Noam Chomsky, he writes, is obviously a genius in linguistics, but seriously unwise when he steps outside of his specialty. Being skilled in one field often leads us to think that we're "intelligent" in other fields too. Chomsky does this with political philosophy, as so do many other so-called intellectuals. Experts in language and literature seem to be disproportionately enamored with Marxism, despite its alarming history of mass-murder. It's sort of a big problem to think you're advocating for the benefit of the downcast and oppressed but end up being the oppressor who slaughters millions just because. Oops. Ideas do indeed have consequences.

All forms of Marxism are the no-touch knockout school of political philosophy. They never work because they violate basic laws of morality (private property being made public, for example, is always theft no matter what you call it). That such brilliant people have fallen for its lies should give us pause and inspire philosophical humility. There is perhaps no more common an occurrence in history than for men and nations doing terrible things based on flawed premises.

It's the same thing here. A categorical fallacy hits Wing Chun when we think that technical knowledge - or knowing the whole system, so to speak - immediately translates to fighting skill. Biu Jee strikes at the heart of martial-snobbery. It eviscerates our thinking that just "holding the center" or something like that literally guarantees combat success.

The truth is that technical precision devoid of tactical skill is like a great race car without a driver. Or it's like a great company with an idiot in charge. Or a monkey with a great tool box. Techniques don't fight by themselves and probably more than other methods these days, Wing Chun fighters need to be reminded of this. Why? Well, because the Wing Chun theory, and the unique beauty of the system , conspire to make us too internal in our focus.

Another point to ponder as we move forward is that in our day and age of specialists - read that: people who *talk about what other people actually do* - there's a natural disconnect between our understanding of theory and practice. It helps us to be careful. A professor of economics often times isn't someone who has ever started and successfully run a business. This isn't to say that theory has no part, or that we should disparage the work of the professor, but that the judge of truth is always application in reality, not the chalkboard, diploma, or instructor certification. Sadly, these things, once achieved, can cause all of us to fall into that categorical fallacy.

BIU JEE CHALLENGES THE "FUNDAMENTALIST" mentality of Wing Chun. But, again, it's only a contradiction if we commit the aforementioned fallacy. It's contradictory if we conflate technical training with application.

So, it's both eye-attacks and defense. But it's generally an attack first since the best defense is a good offense. Nevertheless, what we want in life and what we get are hardly ever the same thing, so both are important.

Biu Jee is teaching us that the Wing Chun fighter, to be logically consistent with the goals of all-out warfare, seeks to attack the weakest targets of the enemy as expeditiously as possible. Wing Chun's philosophy is that of simplicity. True. To achieve simplicity in action one must forswear the common malady of majoring in minors. To that end, there are many things we *can* do…much coolness, yes. But survival is no place for low percentage stuff. There's nothing more simple, direct, and efficacious than taking an eye out and this is why the "advanced" form makes such a big deal about it.

The small mom-and-pop business that's run by a family who loves what they do and does it well, and that's been in business for decades, is a smashing economic success. We never hear about that, nor study it in MBA programs. Isn't that funny? Most of us don't like the soul-sucking nature of corporate life and yet accept the system of lies that leads to it. We say we want simplicity and that we love small business but vote for an ever expanding regulatory state because we fall for the lies of politicians.

Big government hates the "gig" economy but it's the gig - all those independent contractors doing their own thing - that's true success for most people. Most people, if you ask them, would choose to have more freedom and less money rather than lots of money and less freedom (stress). What happens is that politicians, who are in the main philosophically opposed to economic liberty in the first place and prefer some type of command and control structure, demagogue the issue. They infantilize voters. They convince people that they need a mommy in a suit. So, big companies get to write regulations that only "specialists' read (i.e., people whose only skill in life is bossing other people around) and we end up with higher costs and hurdles everywhere.

In other words, this is exactly how complexity creeps in. I'm bringing it up in a Wing Chun book not to make political points but to hammer home the philosophical point. If we're unaware of the virus we'll invariably fall for it in some area of life or another.

The small mom-and-pop literally is good economics. But the masters of complexity, who've never built a business or service that others will freely and gladly trade for, by nature hate simplicity. Since they aren't busy applying themselves to providing a good or service to trade with others, they master the art and craft of rules and regulations. This is how a society dies. When productive men and women need permission from bureaucrats to share their skills, and when they get it they need to pay a tithe to those same so-called "public servants", we know that we live in a lie.

Likewise, when we "take up arms" in a martial art, we're seeking the most logically consistent means of protecting ourselves in the event of unavoidable violence. If we want to box or do MMA we can go do that. But we know self-defense isn't those things. So, the issue is simple. The problem is when, like with economics, martial bureaucrats confuse the issue. The goal becomes something else. The struggle to keep the main thing the main thing is incessant. Simplicity is lost when we fail to be philosophically ruthless. In every endeavor we need to be vigilant.

What's the goal?

Is this necessary to achieve the goal?

Fuzzy thinking…that is, emotionalism…just believing things are true because we like them, is philosophical cowardice. The true master swears off "second-hand" living. The master doesn't conform his/her mind to anything but the truth, the whole truth and nothing but the truth. He isn't, as it's said today, a *philosophical* soy-boy that vacuously trusts others to think for him. He trusts the truth and takes upon himself the arduous task of discovering it.

Biu Jee is confusing to Wing Chun bureaucrats the way that a truly small business is to a corporate philosopher. The small business owner wants to do what they love. They share it with others at a fair price so that they turn enough profit in order to continue to do what they love and do it well. The focus, though, isn't the profit but the skill in which they do the thing they love. The corporate philosophy of growth believes in quality and skill only in service of profit. Profit is the main thing. The difference between the two is this: the goal. An old shipyard in Norfolk, Virginia had their mission statement on a wall. It read:

"WE WILL BUILD GOOD SHIPS. *At a profit if we can, at a loss if we must, but we will build good ships.*"

THAT'S the true economic spirit because only in the free exchange of excellence and skill does one truly serve their neighbor. This is the philosophy of corporatism:

"WE WILL MAKE EVER INCREASING *profit building ships. We will make only as good a ship as necessary to make a profit.*"

IT'S the focus on the main goal that makes all the difference. Great mistakes are made by making small compromises. Thus, if the goal is self-defense we must spend the majority of our training time developing the technique and application reflexes to attack the body's command and control center. Take out the eyes and the rest of the body can't function, right? But what about grappling? It comes into play only insofar as it's needed to serve the aforementioned truth. What about sparring? It's only used as a prescription so that students develop the attributes of timing and accuracy so that they can achieve the central attack plan.

Biu Jee tells us this basic thing but bureaucratic thinking that's focusing on a minor issue rather than the main thing complicates what is simple and direct. We repeat: Wing Chun is an eye attacking method. If this doesn't work, it has a system of simple Plan B's it applies that. For example, if the eye-attack isn't available, the jaw/throat/neck is. If they aren't, the groin is the option. If all of the above are out of play, the knee is good. Why in blazes would you - when your life is literally in the balance - throw an elbow to the head when you could instead eye-gouge? The elbow makes sense only if you quickly come back with an eye attack! That's why you keep seeing that very action in the form. Biu Jee is teaching us that sometimes we're forced to do an auxiliary move. It happens. Fighting is nasty business and the other guy is moving and not cooperating. But no matter what, do what you have to do to survive and get back after those eyes.

Notice it doesn't teach us that we should just do whatever... that's philosophical *nihilism*. Biu Jee is a philosophy degree in a form. It's saying the issue of expediency and the principles of truth are always in play at the same time. Life is both unity and diversity; the truth is one and many. Biu Jee is *principled-pragmatism* in action. Go after that soft target. Do it fast. Do it with consummate skill. Do it ruthlessly like King David taking out Goliath. Wing Chun is the David and Goliath system! But if you need to adjust, make the adjustment. But the adjustment is exactly that...get right back to the main thing after the adjustment. You don't abandon the main thing, you only adapt and then carry on with your primary mission, which is to destroy/degrade your enemy's functional combat capacity.

Sight.

Air.

Mobility.

Simple, but not easy.

So, beware of complexity. Complexity is the devil. It occurs when the minor things obscure the main thing.

Be warned. Be vigilant. And please know that simplicity is the true way of the Christian warrior/philosopher. It's the way of freedom. To live the good life requires non-contradictory identification of meaning (purpose) and action. It requires correct theory and practice. Simplicity in action is integration of the elements (particulars); complexity is produced by both the refusal to state clearly and unambiguously one's core principles and to act consistently with them.

13

Elbows & Jack Reacher

If you're a fan of Lee Child's *Jack Reacher* then you've assuredly noticed that the big man (Reacher), fictional though he is, is nevertheless quite realistic when it comes to fighting. To my knowledge the author is not a Wing Chun man, nor does his professional background show any sort of close-quarter combat training. Despite this, his depiction of real-world combat is chock full of wisdom.

Perhaps the greatest bit of tactical wisdom possessed by the Reacher character is that he neglects punching as part of his close-quarter combat tool kit. Punching, you see, is just a tad bit dangerous for the hands. Many others, my Sifu, Tony Massengill included, completely agree with this.

This is, if you'll indulge the author for a moment, a prime example of the value of an honest-to-goodness system. Because all of us have a tendency to favor those things we find more natural and eschew those that don't come as easily, a systematic keeps us from becoming too one-dimensional. In my case, I've always been drawn to boxing. Punching is something I've learned and relied upon over the years. This isn't to say that good punching technique is purely "natural" as much as it is to say that it's something I've

171

gravitated toward. Certainly there's great study and discipline involved.

A good puncher's downfall might be his very best asset if, in fact, he challenges your elbow with a good punch .

But there's always a bias in all of us. Everyone has their presuppositions and preferences. These aren't bad things in and of themselves so long as we're careful and honest. In fact, such preferences and passions are exactly what makes us unique and human.

The problem is when we confuse preferences with principles.

A principle is a foundational truth in a given category. Principles are both immutable (unchangeable given their categorical context) and foundational - that is, we can't think clearly without them. A preference is downstream of principle. Much vanity and vexation are avoided in human endeavors and interactions if we succeed in not treating one like the other.

For example, my predilection for punching is not a principle. If I confuse this and treat it like a bedrock principle, then I'll hamstring both my own practice and yours. This is why a systematic is vital and why Wing Chun instructors (all teachers at that) must stay philosophically disciplined so as to not impose their own preferences as if they're principles.

On that count, incidentally, Sifu Tony has never demanded that

I alter my approach. Being a professional, he understands that proper punching is taught in the Wing Chun systematic and is, therefore, a logical application tool within the system. He *prefers* other tools such as eye-gouges. Yes, like all of us, he has his preferences and though he's a strong advocate for these preferences he doesn't neglect the responsibility to educate his students (including yours truly) in the principles.

The Biu Jee form provides a Jack Reacher type approach to the challenges presented by all-out violence. It introduces the use of the elbow (*Kop Jarn*) in a manner that seems to contradict the principles of the previous forms. It takes discipline and humility to apprehend the truth of this and avoid errors of logic that eviscerate both our own critical thinking abilities *and* the efficacy of the systematic in question.

DO the hacking elbows violate the centerline principle? Do they violate the economy of motion principle?

Thankfully, no.

There's no "deal with the devil" going on here. Wing Chun is not saying on one hand, "keep the centerline" and on the other, "go ahead and ignore the centerline." The mistake is in thinking that the centerline is a bedrock *tactical* principle - that is, an application principle. It's not! It's a reference point, not a fighting tool. We can't hit someone with the centerline. I know that this is going to hit some readers like an actual elbow to the noggin, but this foolish slavery to the centerline principle is the root of all sorts of application disasters.

Stepping in with simultaneous attack and control.

Remember what we said about a principle? It's a foundational and immutable truth in a *specific category*. A great and common error that plagues us today is the inability to think in categories. The centerline is a structural principle. Structural principles don't fight but we fight with them. If many strikes and tools we use are *types* of Fook-sao, then it's fair to say that strikes that come "over the top" are types of Kop-jarn. Think of an overhand punch, for example.

A technique is a structural foundation of an application tool. The straight punch is a tool. Taan-sao is a tool. Centerline is not a tool and unless we're talking about someone's spinal cord, there's no physical reality to the centerline. This means that it's an abstraction and you can't hit people with an abstraction. You can, however, hit them with an eye-jab or elbow. Centerline is to fighting what furniture is to your living room. The category of "furniture" implies things like chairs and sofas, right? That's understood by one and all. But we get confused when we're talking about more diverse subjects like Wing Chun and violence.

Centerline is the structural principle that helps us see the unity and diversity of economy of motion as well as the body's weakest targets. It's for this reason that we rightly and logically study the centerline principle.

Controlling the centerline, in principle, means, in the main, controlling the offense capacity of the enemy. Many Wing Chun instructors, confused on this point, teach their students that as long as they control the center that all will be well. This is the categorical confusion we're talking about. Wing Chun students who "blast forward" can and do get walloped over the top and around the corner for such foolishness. There's ample evidence of this all over YouTube. So, a wooden interpretation of the principle - out of its categorical context - leads invariably to application difficulties.

A good example of this point is to watch some video of Ip Ching, Edmund Fong, or Tony Massengill doing chi-sao. (You'll see our family's "DNA" in the way they roll, by the way). What you notice is a high level mastery of the relevant principles and techniques in play. What you won't notice is a slavish attempt to always "be on the centerline." Those masters know that the main tactical principle is to control the enemy and let him help you hit him. In other words, they use the relevant principles in order to achieve the primary goal. The main goal is to keep ourselves as safe as possible in the event of unavoidable violence. It isn't to "stick with the guy" or to "control the centerline." Those are derivative principles downstream of the main one.

You see, Ip Ching wasn't doing whatever he felt like. He wasn't ignoring the centerline. He was in control of the enemy. He was using the centerline principle and not being slavishly used by it. What you see when watching such masters is the process of excellence.

LEARN THE PRINCIPLE. *Abide by the principle. Dissolve the principle.*

SO, back to elbows and all that.

The elbow, like all other techniques, is a tool. The form (Biu Jee) gives us the opportunity to learn it. Biu Jee comes along like a coach and says, *"Hey, kid. You're doing great with the basic structure. Good for you. You've devoted the necessary hours to the previous forms and you now have a good sense of your balance and power structure. Now let me show you how to use some tools you probably haven't thought about…or were confused and thought you were prohibited from using."* Wing Chun forms are the physical link to the wisdom of the past. They're a treasured resource in which the voices of the masters of old can whisper in our ear. But, as always, the student can't merely "show up for class" - we must strive to understand those ancient whispers.

The forms are the systematics of structures that keep us, as we said, from becoming too one-dimensional. In fact, if we were to add up all the techniques from the three forms we'd notice that the elbows keep pace with the punches in sheer volume. And this makes sense because Wing Chun purports to be an extremely close-range fighting system. Well, if we're crossing hands with the enemy then the elbow is a nifty little tool and can do things the fists often times find impossible.

And while we're on the subject, we notice that palm strikes (or pushes depending upon the need) are also rather numerous in the Wing Chun systematic. See where this is going? Once we get the structural foundations down - that is, we've developed professional competence - we notice that we have a diversity of useful tools at our disposal.

ARE ELBOWS "BETTER" than punches? Well, that's the thing you and I need to decide for ourselves. They each have their pros and cons and won't apply themselves. Sifu Tony says it perfectly:

"FORMS PROVIDE *the structural foundation of applications that are limited only by your need, unique characteristics, and imagination.*"

FOR SOME OF YOU, the elbows (palms, eye-gouges, etc.) may very well be superior to punching - even if that makes a boxing-loving instructor like me sad. If you're built like Jack Reacher and are able to tie people up and then smash them into oblivion with devastating elbows, that's a good way to go. Good for you. Doing so will not bring the wrath and fury of Wing Chun gods down upon you because you've broken tradition. Respecting tradition and idolatry are a fine line we must be careful not to cross. They only appear similar. One can and should respect the past without being bound by it.

In fact, you may get to the Biu Jee level and then decide that you never want to throw another chain-punch for the rest of your life. You can do that and still do Wing Chun! We aren't talking about skipping the foundations and just coming to Biu Jee. That's laziness and pride. No. What we mean is mastery. It's a high level of skill that has so integrated the foundational skills of Wing Chun into one's DNA that they're always there, running in the background. Your style of application is like an app downloaded on the operating system.

14

Wing Chun Kuen Sum Faat

In another book I wrote, *Wing Chun for the Modern Warrior,* I included a chapter about how hyper-traditionalist thinking makes Wing Chun out to be God. Why? Because logically speaking, the only thing that can be an end in and of itself - that is to say, a context unto itself (or Himself, in this case) is God. A martial art is a *disciplinary art* in that it changes, for the better, the person submitting to and training it. A *Glock* handgun is a literal tool. A hammer is a literal tool. Wing Chun is, as we said, a disciplinary art that uses tools. It's both a concrete thing and an abstraction. As with carpentry, it's art and science. A carpenter uses a tool like a hammer the way a Wing Chun man or woman uses, say, a punch or kick.

What we mean is that a hammer in one's hand, or a Glock, doesn't necessarily change the person. They learn to utilize the tool but they are not the tool itself. A martial art is, in fact, an art as well as a science. Wong Shun Leung is famous for his insistence that Wing Chun isn't an art, but a science. We have to disagree with the incontestably great master on this point. We profess that it's both art and science. To say Ving Tsun/Wing Chun Kuen Sum Faat is to say, "Ving Tsun Fist Heart Law." That's the point. In short, the first two forms teach us about the physics of our body...the law. That's the primary goal of the first form, SLT, especially. By Biu Jee and advanced Chi-Sao, however, we focus more upon the "heart," which is to say the art/mind of combat. Of course, both aspects are always there at all times – art and science, heart and law. It's a matter of focus.

Men and women, in all their diversity of psychology, temperament, and physical gifts, are not mere tools. To say that Wing Chun is a science alone is to say that the study of it turns the man/woman into a tool to be used. That's logically impossible. Human beings are not mere automatons no matter the amount of training. A human being can't be a hammer or a Glock. This theological/philosophical truth regarding the nature of man is the root of Wong Shun Leung's mistake. To regard Wing Chun as a science alone and not an art is to believe that men and women can be *things* and not people.

For this reason, Wing Chun *uses the tools* of one's body like a musician uses a guitar (or some other musical instrument). One learns to play the instrument. They learn the chords and all that. The guitar has a specific nature (laws of logic are always present... in this case the *law of identity*). These laws must be understood, and practice must be undertaken in which the goal is not merely to obey those laws, but to *absorb* them.

Wing Chun is, therefore, the guitar (or bass, if you don't know how to play a real instrument...it's a joke...relax) of violence. A martial artist plays the instruments of *Pak-sao and lop-sao*. People don't usually say, "hey, I know guitar." On the contrary, they say, "I *play* guitar." That's a significant difference. The man who has a hammer or leaf-blower can rightly say that he *knows* that tool insofar as he means that he understands its operational capacity and intent. Yes, he can use it "creatively" to some extent, but the nature of the tool is quite limited. We suppose that a leaf blower can work to blow dry one's hair, but it's hardly optimal.

A guitarist plays. Likewise, a Wing Chun fighter plays.

The structures are the same because the human body (physics) don't change due to our personality or desires. We may have an acoustic guitar or an electric one and there are, of course, a multitude of types across that spectrum. Likewise with the human body. You may be tall or short, fast or slow. But you're still a human being.

But the application of the thing - the guitar or Wing Chun - can and will vary quite a bit. If Wing Chun is merely *"Ving Tsun Kuen Hok"* (Wing Chun fist science) then issues like the environment, terrain/footing, type and number of opponent(s), weapons, legal realities, and all that are irrelevant. What we mean is that gravity doesn't need lawyers. The science of gravity is what it is and there are no congressional hearings on it. You can sue people for use of force. You can't sue gravity (although some enterprising law firm is probably trying to figure out a way to do that as I write this).

Furthermore, there's a significant difference of personal temperament and attributes of the people tasked with applying the art/science. Trying to make Mike Tyson fight like Floyd Mayweather, or vice versa, would ruin both. Tyson's *style* of boxing was specific to him. The peek-a-boo and the Philly-shell fit the men using them - their physical *and* psychological qualities.

This is all to say that the way *you play* Wing Chun should and must be unique to you. That's the whole point. The physics (the science) are the same but the people using them vary in significant ways. To this end we return to the definition of Wing Chun as a *disciplinary art* rather than a mere tool. To be clear, a disciplinary art - a creative discipline - is, as Bruce Lee said it, expressed by the individual using it. There's an integration of the elements when the tool meets the man. If a Wing Chun man or woman is but a scientific fact and not a living, breathing martial *artist*, then one must wonder why not be a soldier instead.

The mystery of martial arts is in the fact that it is indeed both art and science. The mystery is in the unique interplay of the objective and the subjective. It's neither one or the other, but both. Philosophers refer to this as the issue of the "one and the many." The term "university" comes from the knowledge that reality is both "unity and diversity."

The Wing Chun *artist* is like the musical guitarist...or drummer or vocalist. The musician has a specialty of instrument and yet is a student (disciple - that is, disciplined learner) of music. A very skilled guitarist is skilled in a particular way such as rock or country or classical. He/she might play in a band or maybe they're a session musician. Though there's a risk of belaboring the point we believe that the stakes are so high (considering that we're talking about violence) that it's essential we get it right.

A boxer or MMA enthusiast is a student of a particular form of warfare. It's the same with the Wing Chun player. All parties are students of war, so to speak. But the thing about Wing Chun is that it's a broader discipline than sport combat due to the reality of all-out violence and its many variables. This is where so many of us get lost.

There's a common thought that the reason Wing Chun has fallen into some disrepute as of late - at least compared to the afore-mentioned combat sports - is because the Wing Chun students aren't sparring. Though this is somewhat true, it's true because its teachers are philosophically confused on this particular point. A martial artist recognizes the diverse and broad nature of combat. A boxer doesn't necessarily need to do that because his/her focus is more strictly applied. The reality of violence is an extraordinary topic. It covers philosophy and ethics as well as physics and tactics.

So, yes, on one level we can accurately say that Biu Jee deals with "emergency" techniques. We can say that it helps us "escape" problems. But this is not all that it is. More still, such thinking tends to make us the aforementioned *Winchesters* of Wing Chun. Winchesters are known by their erroneous belief that the battle is won by controlling the centerline or by the perfection of one's chi-sao. They confuse technical skill and mechanics with the reality of brutal combat. They obsess about the first two forms and the primary drills. The Kop-Jarn elbows become, therefore, nothing more than escapes rather than actually useful weapons/tools. And it makes sense too. If centerline is *the* thing...if it's a weaponized principle rather than merely a refer-ence point, then it becomes the standard of one's application. And if that's the case, whipping one's elbows over the top is like seeing the Pope in a thong. It's all wrong. (Sorry for that mental image, but you get the point).

The bottom line of Wing Chun is that it's a self-defense tool, not the goal itself. This is a *philosophical truth* that precedes and interprets the scientific data downstream of it. All facts must be interpreted; context is king. The goal of self-defense is to keep ourselves as safe as possible in the event of unavoidable violence. The forms provide the structural foundations of applications (techniques). The drills provide the necessary repetitions that yield "fighting reflexes (because knowing isn't enough...we have to apply the material under pressure). Application in a diverse environment against diverse opponents by unique individuals is the idea of *looking beyond the pointing finger.* It's the stuff of creative adaptation to the facts of reality in the service of the aforementioned goal. If you're good at elbows or kicks or punches, or whatever else, seek to maximize your advantages. Likewise, by the time you finish Biu Jee you have a good idea of what your weaknesses are too. The idea is to develop your strengths so that they supersede your limitations in the goal of self-defense.

Wing Chun won't fight for you. As we've pointed out, the goal is to use it rather than to be used by it. The minute we get into thinking "you can't do that" we've arrived at a place of issuing ethical commandments over tactical applications. It's clearly not a technical commandment, right? I mean, if someone says, "you can't sprawl in Wing Chun" they don't mean that technically because clearly the human body can and does sprawl. What they're saying is that it's not permissible *tactically.* It's an ethical commandment. Watch for it. This is how we detect when we've crossed that line between talking about self-defense and religion. One may very well say, "that's not the most efficient way to do that." The issue then is one of practical application and use. But to say that one literally cannot, is a blurring of the philosophical lines of tactics and ethics.

God gets to issue ethical proclamations, not men. And this is precisely where Biu Jee proves how brilliant Wing Chun truly is. It shows that Wing Chun's emphasis on logical structure (in the previous forms) isn't meant as a chain, but as a foundation and guide. Indeed, it shows that we can learn the principle, practice (abide by) the principle, and then dissolve the principle. We all get the same material because we're all human beings (i.e., we're bound by certain laws of physics) but those rules are guides, not shackles. You might kick like lightning; I might paak-sao and punch like Bruce Lee. Either way, the goal is to apply our strengths and avoid our weaknesses while shutting down the enemy.

Thus, don't settle for less than mastery, which means that you're going to have to think and train seriously. You're going to have to soberly assess yourself throughout your journey. Biu Jee isn't about merely the weaknesses of the system but about our own. A theory doesn't fight (or live) for us; we do. What weaknesses have you encountered and what's your plan to address them? What great strengths do you have that you aim to maximize in combat (and life, for that matter).

Mastery in this context, be sure, doesn't mean perfection. People get really hung up on this and there's all sorts of fanboy nonsense attached to it. Who cares if Ip Man could have beaten such and such…who cares if Bruce Lee was better than Tyson. We need to jettison all that drivel and balderdash that clogs up the online forums and focus on the truth of our training…of what we can and can't do. By Biu Jee level you shouldn't be copying anyone anymore! As Oscar Wilde said:

"Imitation is the sincerest form of flattery that mediocrity can pay to greatness."

You now have the core material and philosophy of looking beyond the pointing finger. It's up to you to not stop there and actually apply the lessons to yourself. What others have done can be an inspiration, sure, but by this point you should know well that you can't copy. To go back to the guitar analogy: you need to write your own song now.

15

Self Defense: the unknown
ideal

Self-defense is the bedrock principle of human society. Since none of us are God, no one has the right to play God over anyone else. Since none of us are God, no one has the right to issue ethical proclamations that bind our neighbors. Only God is God and that's why the principle of self-defense is true *and absolutely essential* for peace. Peace is not the absence of frustration; peace is the absence of the initiation of force against those who are minding their own business. Peace is when all interactions are conducted on a voluntary basis toward a win-win goal *and* self-defense is recognized as the moral use of force to repel an immoral initiation of force…that is, the denial of choice.

No society can be moral if it jettisons the concept of self-defense because there's no such thing as a moral vacuum. Life requires choices and these choices must be made by individuals according to their best reasoning in pursuit of their personal goals. Since no one can know the entirety of another person - past, present and future - no one is qualified, nor morally authorized, to choose for another adult. To be human is to be a "chooser" and this means that the denial of choice is that which dehumanizes, i.e., is a violation of rights.

Frustration, poverty, pain, etc., are adverse qualities of life in a fallen (therefore, imperfect) world but unless they're the direct result of the denial of one's choice by another, they aren't unethical. A tree fell on a man's house during a storm recently, thus ruining his house and severely injuring the man. This wasn't an unethical action because the tree had no choice. There can be no violation of morality unless choice is abridged. The ethical component of the use of defensive force is that it must only be directed at the *personal* initiator of the dehumanizing aggression.

The principle teaches that the use of violence, threat of violence (coercion), or fraud, is the act of playing God over someone insofar as it steals from them their humanity. Violence, coercion, and fraud all deny the consent of the neighbor and that's precisely why it's evil. No person is authorized to deny another human being their God-given right to their own mind - that is, their consent. This means that the only right is the right to choose one's own course. No right can exist that removes frustration because that must necessarily include the denial of consent from others. No one has a right to something supplied by another person no matter how desperate the need.

Human suffering and vexation can and should be met by love and charity. But charity can't be forced. No earthly expedient supersedes the moral law of consent. The moral law of self-defense logically prohibits the use of force - i.e., the denial of choice - against all but the initiator of evil.

The principle of self-defense, therefore, teaches that this sacred right of consent is the lone reason for which we may morally justify the use of force. Violence may only be used in defense of one's essential freedoms. Essential freedoms are those things which one must rely upon to live and are primary to us as image-bearers of God. These are: the authority of our body, our labor, and our property.

The usurpation of any one of these entails the denial of all of them. Consequently, freedom is rendered null and void whenever these are in any way abridged. And they can only be abridged if one's choice is stolen.

The use of violence to defend these essential freedoms is, therefore, not only permissible, but morally good because to confuse the issue is to elevate evil over good. Never can the evisceration of consent be said to be good. Oh, how much evil and horror have been perpetrated by those who ignore so simple a truth!

For example, a man can't get out of his car and beat the bejabbers out of a dude who made him miss a red light. That's an inconvenience, be sure. Maybe the offending fellow drives worse than my mother-in-law (pure fantasy, I assure you, because even a cadaver drives faster than her) but that's not an issue of essential freedom. Clearly frustrating…like rooting for the Cowboys in the playoffs, yes, but not a violation of rights.

On the other hand, a carjacking *is* a violation of essential freedom. If someone can literally stop you from going someplace and/or take your property, especially something as important as your primary means of transportation, then they've made you their slave. This is what crime is, in fact.

Do you know what the difference between a mugger and a politician is? The scale of their theft.

It's always and forever immoral to deny consent whether you do it in Congress or on a street corner with a gun.

You see, the principle of self-defense is the literal antidote to chaos, conflict, and bloodshed in society. Everyone knows it to be true, but the issue is whether we have the moral courage to follow the principle and apply it consistently. Sadly, history shows us (and recent experience too) that as soon as people are frustrated or scared, they will ruthlessly abridge the freedom of their neighbors. This goes to show us that the vast majority speak of freedom but they really mean comfort. Society will never know true peace or justice until it understands and has the honesty to follow the true principles of liberty. Indeed, few words are more misunderstood.

WITH THIS SAID, we turn back to our issue at hand, which is Wing Chun and Biu Jee.

It's a technical marvel, be sure. It's a piece of scientific savagery hiding in plain sight and it's this savagery, be sure, that required this preamble. The lessons of Biu Jee will be utterly and completely lost to us if we don't understand the truth it's pointing to, which is the all-out nastiness of self-defense. Biu Jee is there so that we maximize our self-defense capabilities under the worst kind of pressure: deadly pressure. To see it as merely a "form" is to commit the mistake of focusing on the proverbial finger while ignoring what it's pointing at. In this case, it's not the moon, but the trench warfare of combat.

To that end we've said and shown some tough things indeed. This is no game. I've lost plenty of games. My son recently beat the dickens out of me playing basketball. In my defense, by the way, I'm in my mid-50's, and he's 18. It doesn't help that he's also about six inches taller too. And the sun was in my eyes. A lot. And I had a bit of a cold that day too. But, anyway, I lost badly, yes. If people had been watching they might have been moved to tears (of sadness or laughter depending upon their sensitivities, of course). Nevertheless, I got up the next morning with nary a recollection of that epic beatdown.

But that's absolutely not the case with a fight, is it?

To lose at violence is life-altering or life-ending. I certainly wouldn't be making jokes about losing at violence so soundly, would I? Can you imagine making rape or murder jokes?

A FIGHT IS A SAVAGE THING. It's easy to forget that due, thankfully, to the relative security and peace we've experienced in recent history. But this history is rather an anomaly. Life is not, be sure, all sunshine and moonlit beaches. Ever since Cain beat Abel's brains in with a rock, and Lamech wailed on some poor soul for insulting him, mankind's history has run rivers of red, red blood.

The misunderstanding of the 2nd Amendment largely stems from this softness of prolonged peace. It's convinced us that mankind doesn't have a problem with evil aggression and, therefore, that being armed and ready for warfare is some relic of the barbaric past. Lattes and iPhones have certainly made life more comfortable but they haven't altered human nature. No matter how cozy and warm we might be, the basics of humanity remain unaltered.

Nicholas Murray Butler (1862-1947), the former president of Columbia University, is a wonderful example of the hubris of modernity. Convinced that war and strife could be eradicated by education, Butler imagined a time when naval warships would instead be educational crafts, bringing books and charity rather than bombs. A few years after this vacuous prognostication, the First World War was in full swing and boys were being blown asunder all over mud-filled fields in Europe. And yet even that experience didn't sway him.

Later, in 1941, when the Pulitzer Prize fiction jury selected Hemingway's *For Whom the Bell Tolls* as its winner for that year, the Pulitzer board agreed. Hemingway gets it.

Oh, but wait.

Murray found Hemingway's masterpiece of the Spanish Civil War to be offensive. Or too salacious. Or whatever. We aren't exactly sure. In any event, the earth didn't move when he read it. Stories of war behind enemy lines, passion, betrayal, love, sex, and death really can't be done much better than *Papa's* depiction, yet Murray apparently didn't like the subject matter. Being the *ex officio* head of the board, he persuaded them to reverse its decision. No Pulitzer was awarded for fiction that year.

The reality of men like Murray is that they're convinced, against an avalanche of evidence to the contrary, that mankind doesn't have a sin/aggression problem. In their estimation it's something else... and that's always the putrid seed from which all conflict grows. Murray was blind to the evil of Hitler and Mussolini for the same reason that modern leftists are easily seduced by the totalitarian charms of socialistic pipe-dreams. They confuse their earnestness with truth. They're like a child looking out the window and wishing that January was June. When we become convinced that mankind's essential problem isn't inside of us, that it's something lurking outside, we have a problem. A violent one. *Out there* always means other people no matter how we dress it up...the system, the way it is, privilege, the bourgeoise, *kulaks*, the Jews. Murray and his intellectual allies always miss the scapegoating that tyrants do because they reject the principle of self-defense and the truth of rights it rests upon. They miss it because in their intellectual vanity, they intend to be rulers…they intend that others will be pacified to live by their "grand" ideas. They never see themselves as oppressors because they never have the personal courage, nor skill, to do it themselves.

The refusal to swear off the use of force/regulation against others, for any reason (and especially "good" reasons) is the root of all conflict, violence and war. The fans of good literature are just as capable of tyranny and violence as people who think that mud-wrestling and mosh pits are high entertainment. *There can be no logical or moral reason to ever violate the rights of other people or logic and morality don't exist.* This principle alone is the foundation of peace. Force can only be applied - morally, that is - in direct defense of one's rights. Frustration is not a violation of our rights or else the rapist and the mugger are morally justified. If the other person can't disagree with you, if they can't ignore you and/or walk away, you're the aggressor. You're the problem.

This and only this (the principle of self-defense) provides a logically consistent social ethic as well as the moral fences needed to understand and restrain the use of force.

Note this well: men like Murray speak incessantly of peace but never of self-defense. Why? For the simple reason that they intend to rule others. Persuasion is the "weapon" of the free man or woman. The criminal uses brute force; the successful tyrant uses the perverted law of tyrannical states. The dividing line between right and wrong, insofar as social ethics are concerned, is always choice and its handmaiden, self-defense.

But whereas the mugger and rapist intend to rule at the point of the knife, or the barrel of the gun, such "educated" men (and women, of course) will rule by their sophistry. The result is "organized" oppression. Guns, force, and threat of force dominate and the sophists rule behind them. Why would they get their hands dirty when others are always willing to do their bloody work for them, right?

In our day we've seen the triumph of the utopian-bullies.

Freedom - as in: all people have a right to self-defense - is the modern unicorn. Everywhere the principle of self-defense articulated here is unknown; its implications never followed.

The power of this argument is its brutal simplicity and that's exactly why no tyrant or bully wants to talk about it. Our "betters" and our "elites" moan incessantly about what they call misinformation when, in fact, everything they say in regard to ethics and politics are exactly that. Like a man with a mistress in his bedroom telling his wife in the kitchen that he loves her is the person who speaks of peace while ignoring the true principle of self-defense.

Critics of the 2nd Amendment and concealed carry like to say that it's intended for the collective militia, not individuals. There's a great intellectual sleight of hand in that because it was individuals who literally were the militia. Citizens living on a frontier weren't calling 911 when the Indians or bandits attacked and killed the men *and* the women and children. They fought for their own defense prior to the collective militia going to exact vengeance.

This whole life being sunshine and moonbeams has filtered into the interpretation of Wing Chun too. It's neutered the scientific savagery of its unique combat philosophy and nowhere do we see that better exemplified than in Biu Jee's emphasis on eye attacks. That chain punching is considered the staple and identifying aspect of Wing Chun to the masses rather than jabbing, raking, or gouging the eyes - from afar or within the clinch - is testimony to our point. Punching a dude is fine. Hitting his eye is as far superior to a punch as a car is to a bicycle.

A large reason for the misunderstandings surrounding modern Wing Chun, and sport combat too, is that we've altogether suppressed the moral and philosophical purposes of martial art. Modern man is a marvel of inconsistency and contradiction. Outside of him there are astonishing advancements all around... technologically he stands upon mountains. Inside of him, however, he regresses, he succumbs, and kneels in fetid fields of immoral paganism, barbarity and sensuality. We have satellites up in the stars but our minds are in revolting gutters of moral filth. We have access to millions of books, they're alive at our fingertips, and yet we degenerate into the abyss of savagery and addictions as our young destroy their minds watching inane and featherbrained *TikTok* shorts.

America's inner cities, drug-riddled, look like war zones overrun by zombies...and we pass by them...or desist altogether...and try and forget that these are human beings out there living like rats on the streets. We call ourselves advanced because we have technology outside while our minds rot away inside due to our addictions to pleasure. We see freedom not as a pathway to personal achievement through discipline, nor as a way to serve through excellence, but as a doorway to a house of dissipation and lechery.

To that end we say that the martial artist is the one who understands that life's war starts in oneself and takes that responsibility seriously. A fireman may put out a thousand infernos but if he starts only one, he's an arsonist, not a fireman anymore. Such it is here. To speak of the barbarity of combat without the necessity of moral principles guiding the actions - restraining as well as informing them - renders us no higher than that fallen firefighter. The very knowledge of combat's cruelty requires the equal knowledge of one's own responsibility. That Biu Jee's inherent maliciousness, refined and yet so very terrible in its execution, is missed by many, is, oddly enough, due to our suppression of the reality of evil.

Traditionalists love the science and even the combative elegance of Wing Chun and yet recoil at the simple cruelty of real application. To grab a guy, gouge his eyes, head-butt him, slap him in the groin, and then throw him to the floor, is, in their estimation, too vulgar a show. A Wing Chun man ought to be more, well, sophisticated than that. Spit and blood and snot are the stuff of obscenity and the traditionalist doesn't like all that stuff. He gets into Wing Chun to avoid getting dirt under his nails. How much more so blood? Chi-sao is a gentleman's game, he convinces himself, and he intends to live in a world of make-believe that's not red in tooth and claw and where sin hasn't brought a universal death penalty.

Sport combat enthusiasts, on the other hand, decry the fact that they haven't "seen it work in the cage." They're hard pragmatists who "believe it when they see it" and they can't bring themselves to think,. Period. They act and they think such action is thinking. They relegate violence to the square circle or the octagon and refuse to think any deeper than that. Speak to them of Plato or ethics or epistemology and they think that has as much to do with violence as Beethoven. Speak to them of eye-gouging and all that nasty stuff and they retreat to that pragmatism that guides them. The UFC fighter and the boxer contend with the normalcy bias just like the rest of us.

But the true martial artist seeks to lay hold of the *principled* truth. The traditionalist conveniently forgets that his ancestors *fought and died* with these things he practices in nice uniforms in an air-conditioned school. He suppresses the obvious, which is mankind's great scourge. He doesn't like the fact that all-out combat is a bloody, nasty mess and that Leung Jan would certainly have known that. And the sport fighter doesn't want to reckon with the fact that winning a match and winning at life aren't the same thing. It's lack of self-control and respect that cause conflicts, not lack of a good ground game or cardio. A sport fighter who has no concern with the causes of violence is no more a martial artist than me swimming in the lake makes me a fish. A martial artist is one who's both prepared for the stark realities of violence and a lover of wisdom (philosopher) who cherishes the true moral law and intends to live by it through the grace of God. He/she detests not only violence and oppression but the little immoralities and contradictions that proceed from them. In this way only can a martial artist be said to be both mind and body.

Acknowledgments

Sifu Aaron is an amazing martial artist, leader, and teacher. It's been an inestimable blessing to watch him grow over all these years.

The wonderful Academy family has in no wise been fully represented in these pages. Some are camera shy and there are only so many photos we can include. To that end, we'd like to thank our whole Academy family - near and far - and especially those who appeared herein.

Who wants to hit this guy??? Well, judging from the photos, everyone. But, seriously, Rob is one of the best guys you'll ever meet and train with. Everyone loves being partnered with him.

Rob, Glenn, Beth, CW, David and Sadie are incredible martial artists and people too. There's never a bad day here. It seems that every time we turn the lights off and lock the door that we're all laughing and sweating and can't wait for tomorrow. Such is a blessing that this humble writer doesn't take for granted.

Beth is an amazing lady and dedicated martial artist.

I'd also like to thank Aaron for providing the awesome cover to this volume and all his tireless devotion to the craft - both Wing Chun and teaching. He's grown to be an extraordinary warrior-scholar who greatly blesses all who train here. It's been an extraordinary blessing and privilege to watch him grow in Christ as a man as well as to witness him mature as a martial artist as well.

A bright future awaits this young man, Eli. The cool thing
is that his father, Rusty, was one of my very first students
30 years ago. I know…I know…that means I'm getting
old. But no worries. Young men like Eli will be there to
protect me when I get too old.

For information on attending classes online or even becoming a coach/instructor in our lineage, please visit:

Greenville-academy.teachable.com

For more information on our physical kwoon (school) as well as to check out our totally free blog:

greenvilleacademy.com

About the Author

Jason Korol is a life long martial artist, beginning his Wing Chun training in 1981 (right after the dinosaurs died off and the last ice age melted) when his older brother, Michael, came home for Christmas break and summarily slapped him around. Since then he's been training consistently. The author of over a dozen books, and a regular columnist in *Wing Chun Illustrated*, he's a born Yankee (in Upstate New York) but a Southerner by choice. Now that so many Yankees have followed him and traffic is bad, he's considering moving back. Just kidding.

He lives in the upstate of South Carolina where he writes and teaches at Greenville Academy of Martial Arts. He's been married to his long suffering wife, Christine, for 25 years and together they've raised a wise and humble young man who's going off to college. That makes Jason an empty nester, so expect a few more books in the future.

Also, for what it's worth, Jason is an avid baseball, classic rock, and Toyota Tundra fan (the old V8, that is…not that squirrelly and totally unreliable twin turbo V6 monstrosity they call a Tundra). When he's not writing, teaching, training, or at a baseball game, he's up in those glorious Blue Ridge Mountains or down at the beach. Take your pick.

Jason at his home away from home down on the magical South
Carolina coast where so much of his writing is done.

Also by Jason Korol

JKD's Way of the Blade

JKD Infighting

Jeet Kune Do Foundations

Wing Chun Wooden Dummy

Wing Chun's Foundation: Siu Lim Tao

Chum Kiu: Wing Chun's Art of War

Chi Sao: the Genius of Wing Chun

Wing Chun Applications: From the School to the Street

Jeet Kune Do Pure & Simple

Wing Chun for the Modern Warrior

Christ & Self Defense

Printed by Amazon Italia Logistica S.r.l.
Torrazza Piemonte (TO), Italy

68670869R00127